M000249069

From the Top

From the Top
The Dolph Traymon Story

A MEMOIR

The Round House Press
Kent, Connecticut

Copyright © 2012 Dolph Traymon
All rights reserved.

Published by
The Round House Press
PO Box 744
Kent, Connecticut 06757
TheRoundHousePress.com

First Edition: December 2012
ISBN 978-0-9823089-6-7

Library of Congress Cataloging-in-Publication Data
Library of Congress Control Number 2012953277
Traymon, Dolph.
From the top : the Dolph Traymon story : a memoir /
Dolph Traymon. — 1st ed. — Kent, Conn. : Round House Press, c2012.
p. ; cm.
ISBN: 978-0-9823089-6-7
Summary: The memoir of a pianist with a long and distinguished musical history.
From Julliard to Harry James and Frank Sinatra, from Peggy Lee to an Army band,
this is the story of Traymon's extraordinarily vibrant life.—Publisher.
1. Traymon, Dolph. 2. Pianists—United States—Biography. 3. Musicians—
United States—Biography. 4. Big band music—United States. 5. Popular music—
United States. 6. Restaurateurs—Connecticut—Kent.   I. Title.
ML417.T73   T73   2012   2012953277
786.2/092—dc23   1212

Cover and Interior Design by John Labovitz
The text is set in Erhardt, designed in 1937 by Monotype, after Dutch-style types
from the 1700s. It was often used in books from the 1940s to the 1960s.

Front cover photo, Dolph Traymon in 1946, by Bruno of Hollywood for GEM
Records. Back cover illustration depicts the Dolph Traymon Trio at Atlantic City's
Senator Hotel in 1948.

Dedication

WE HAVE COME TO KNOW AND LOVE so many of our devoted customers at the Fife 'n Drum over the years and we enjoy so many warm,
wonderful, and lasting friendships with them. Penny and Ernie Sch-
mutzler, Georgeanne Kent, Tom Sebring and Steve Vaughn have
been staunch supporters of the Fife, as it is affectionately called, as
have Susi and Dick Wyman, who were introduced to each other at our
restaurant.

I dedicate this book to our family, to these dear friends, and to all
who have allowed us to feel so at home at the Fife 'n Drum, every
single day since 1973.

Contents

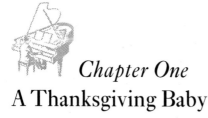

Chapter One
A Thanksgiving Baby

NO LIFE IS MORE FULFILLING than a musical life, and I've had a long and fascinating one. Every day since I was a little child I've made the choice to spend time playing the greatest musical compositions in the world—from Chopin to Cole Porter and Coltrane to *Carousel.* My life's been full of exciting people, many of them famous, most of them deservedly so. I've played and conducted the upbeat swing music that brought us through the War, and I've serenaded lovers in quiet cafes.

Playing the piano has brought me everything, including my beloved Audrey.

I have never failed to be grateful for the magical life I've been given, maybe because I was born on Thanksgiving Day November 27, 1919 at 366 Broome Street in lower Manhattan. My sister, Adele, my brother, Joseph, and I were all born there.

I was a stocky kid, and my brother and sister, when they wanted to be annoying, would call me "Fatty Arbuckle" after that era's popular—later infamous—screen star, who was aptly named.

It's said that I resemble the Cacciaguida side of the family, my mother's people. That side of the family has a fascinating yet mysterious history, which was detailed after much research in the late eighties by Adele, who pointed out that we were born straddling two centuries—the twentieth was just beginning to make progress while the vestiges of the nineteenth lingered on.

I'll let Adele describe the way we grew up:

We were born into a most unusual family with a zest for living. We thrived on good humor and camaraderie. Socializing was a way of life, and music was the heartbeat of all our activities.

Grandfather's Mysterious Origins

Giuseppe Cacciaguida Panuccio, my grandfather, was born on October 3, 1864, and that's all we know for sure. From an oil painting we have in the family, we can observe that he was a very handsome, mustachioed man of fair complexion, fine features, and blue eyes. At the time he sat for the portrait, his hair was gray. The family is full of tales about him.

He was raised by foster parents many miles from where he was born, and for unknown reasons he sometimes preferred to use their surname, Panuccio, that is, when he wasn't using Cacciaguida. This can still be confusing. For instance, his sons were registered in school as Panuccio, but when they were drafted into WWI, they reverted to the name Cacciaguida.

The family believes that Grandfather was born in Florence. We suspect that his mother was from a high station in life, even from nobility, and that his father held an important status in the Catholic Church. There are several reasons for this assumption. He traveled to Florence—always alone—once or twice a year, but never spoke to anyone about those trips. He was distrustful of priests and it upset him when our mother went to confession, or had anything to do with the Church.

Soon after Grandfather was born, he was given to a childless couple in Scilla to raise as their own. Now if you look at a map of Italy you'll see that Florence is near the top of the boot while Scilla is in the toe. That's about as far away from Florence as you can get and still be in Italy.

Scilla is a small, picturesque town in the province of Calabria at the southern end of Italy. Homer writes about it in his Odyssey. Greece founded numerous cities in the area around Scilla and many of these places have retained their Greek names. The Greek language colored local speech and became part of the idiom. Though my grandmother spoke the local Italian dialect, she read and wrote in Greek.

The Mystery Deepens

In Scilla, considerable money and property were provided for Grandfather's upbringing and education. He was reared as a gentleman of leisure, living the good life of a pampered youngster, later hunting and sporting. In his youth he was a gentleman of leisure.

In 1959 my cousin Iris went to Scilla to try to unravel the mystery of Grandfather's origins. Not only were the original records missing, but she also found that the remaining records had been altered, and even the property that had once belonged to Grandfather had been acquired by others. After spending a full month researching in the area, Iris could find nothing that shed light on the subject.

Adele also discovered information missing on legal documents. As she put it in her family memoir, "The conundrum remains. Perhaps it was just as well. Grandpa kept his secret."

But that wasn't all that was to mystify us. The family had long believed that Grandfather was a descendent of the medieval poet Dante Alighieri, Italy's Shakespeare, known as the father of the Italian language. Dante's *The Divine Comedy* is considered important, not just for its literary value, but also for the information he provides about Florence in the twelfth century. The great poet and philosopher, who also studied music and art, claimed that his family descended from the ancient Roman founders of Florence. He wrote about his great-great-grandfather, Cacciaguida degli Elisei (c.1091–c.1148), an Italian crusader born in Florence who took part in Saint Bernard of Clairvaux's crusade of 1147 and died in the Holy Land. He was later declared a martyr by the Church. The early Cacciaguida forecasts Dante's exile from Florence and the solitude of his later years. Cacciaguida and Dante lived to the same age, fifty-six. Cacciaguida was, of course, my grandfather's name.

Grandfather's Old-Fashioned Education

I was not a particularly mischievous kid, but Adele and Joe were, and that tendency was probably handed down from my Florentine grandfather. Here's one story about him.

Grandfather didn't take his school lessons seriously, and after he skipped his assignment yet another time, his tutor felt he should be disciplined. Knowing this was inevitable, the next time Grandfather saw his tutor he made sure to fill his back pockets with ripe prickly pears. When the tutor predictably started to whip his backside, the pears burst and deep red juice flowed. Seeing what he thought was blood, the poor tutor panicked.

His tutor didn't give up on him, however, and Grandfather managed to master the classic languages and French, which was of enormous benefit to him later on, since Scilla's silkworm farms produced raw silk. Once a year, Grandfather went to Lyon and Paris as a silk merchant.

The property Grandfather owned produced abundant olives, figs, and grapes. He raised goats, mainly for the milk used in cheese. One of the varieties of black olives grown on the land was as small as a pinky fingernail; its oil was used in medicine.

A Marriage Arranged to Last

Grandfather married Giovanna Arlotta in 1886 in Scilla. He was twenty-two; she was twenty-five, daughter of Rocco Arlotta and Maria Bellantoni. Typical of the time, it was an arranged marriage but apparently a happy one that produced six children. She came from a well-established Scilla family with four daughters and a son. She was

4

both respected and popular, and blessed with the ability to take command of a situation and see it through. Maria was generous, kind, and apparently very sensitive.

Later, while living in New York, she happened on a slaughterhouse and never ate meat again. That didn't stop her from being an excellent cook who never failed to prepare plenty of extra food. Grandmother was always sending food to someone, somewhere. No surprise that their home was the gathering place for the people of Scilla, who were called Scillesi. They would not only welcome guests for dinner but also would entertain them overnight, with people sleeping double or even triple in the beds.

While coming to the United States was an upward movement for most families, we're not so sure that was the case for ours. After all, Grandfather was leaving a very good life and productive land for an uncertain future. Adele wrote about this in her family memoir.

Why Leave His Land of Plenty?

"Was my grandfather right in uprooting and transplanting his family to America? In retrospect, I wonder. It was not the land of opportunity in comparison to his resources in his native country. Their lifestyle was diminished, and they no longer lived as landed gentry, with servants to attend them.

"For his children, the relocation was a calamity; their education was interrupted and curtailed, and they dissolved into the melting pot of America. By running away from his parentage, he left property, income, and heritage in Italy. He abandoned his birthright, forfeiting all to his foster parents. This relinquished property produced sufficient income to educate the five sons of his foster father, who had remarried after his wife's death. Three of them became doctors, one an engineer, and one a lawyer.

"For Grandpa's children, the relocation was all in vain—the result did not justify the sacrifice."

5

Nevertheless, Grandfather came to the United States in 1900, taking the two oldest boys with him. The exodus from Italy was particularly hard on my mother. The arrangement was that the rest of the family was to arrive in New York the following year. Grandmother, however, used the immigrant quota to bring her sister with her, which meant that one family member had to be left behind for an additional year. When Grandfather met his family at the pier, he was furious when he found out that one of his children had been left behind.

My Mother's Lifelong Scars

My mother, Marie Elsie Cacciaguida, born on February 12, 1892 in Scilla, was the child left behind. Though Grandfather appealed to the authorities to allow her to join the rest of them immediately, she had to wait with her mother's parents for a full year before she could be with her family in their new land. Though her grandparents loved her and treated her very well, she often cried herself to sleep during that year. She was only eight years old.

My mother suffered all her life from the memory of that abandonment.

When she finally did get to sail to America, a married couple from Scilla were also sailing, and she was happily placed in their care. It didn't work out very well, however, because their quarters were on a different deck, where she was not allowed. She was given a bunk in steerage and had to fend for herself for ten days among strangers. Because she passed her time mostly on deck, watching the ocean, she was suntanned to an extraordinary degree.

Poor Mama went through Ellis Island alone, after changing to the clothes she had been told to wear when she was picked up at the dock in America. Grandpa was waiting at the dock for his daughter, but did not recognize her, since she had gotten so dark. After that experience, she never went out in the sun again, as long as she lived, without being covered up.

An Unforgettable Jelly Doughnut

Grandfather hugged and kissed his long-lost daughter and, to comfort her, bought her a jelly doughnut—her first—on the way home. She never forgot that jelly doughnut. Moreover, her terrible experience of being left behind left her with a strong longing for family unity. For the rest of her life, nothing in the world would ever be able to separate her from her children. My mother's devotion to us knew no bounds.

My mother grew up to be a good-looking woman of medium height and build with chestnut-colored wavy hair. Valiant, courageous, and stalwart, she had a zest for life that never left her, and a wonderful singing voice. To my anti-clerical grandfather's obvious dismay, she was Monsignor Kearney's favorite soloist at Old St. Patrick's Church in Lower Manhattan.

Somehow her mother, my grandmother, had the idea that she would be returning to Italy in a short time, so she left her home, linens and all, intact back in Italy. They never did return, however.

The family settled in a new building at 126 Elizabeth Street in lower Manhattan.

A Full Calendar of Family Celebrations

Adele once put together an annual calendar of the typical gatherings and activities enjoyed by our extended family. Looking back at it now, our holiday times seem to represent the simple, innocent family fun, the food, the music, the games, and the laughter that nobody seems to have time for anymore. These were the traditions my family brought over from Europe, as so many others did, too—entertainment that required nothing but the ability to relax, and the love that a good family has for each other. Oh, yes, and plenty of food. As Adele put it, "There was no rivalry among us; we were a phalanx. We were never taught the meaning of love—we were surrounded by it, and so we

7

learned to love one another."

Summer was always the most fun. On July 4, there would be a family picnic on Uncle Pete's lawn, followed by fireworks. We would be going to the beach so frequently that Uncle Joe installed benches along the inside of his truck to accommodate all of us. August was the time for us to pick wild cherries from Aunt Concetta's wild cherry trees. The young children climbed to the upper branches to harvest cherries and everyone helped to pit them. They were then cooked into syrup and jam, enough to last the entire year. When added to ice-cold water, the syrup created a delicious drink we called "Amarena."

On Labor Day weekend we had our last get-together for the summer, and in October, Uncle Joe would bring home boxes of grapes to his wine press. He would draw the first wine and give it to the women, who would make a tasty pudding called "Mustarda." On Halloween, there was a children's party when we bobbed for apples.

In November the family would receive a crate from the property in Italy, with oil, tiny black olives, raisins, and dried baked figs. The crate also would include Torrone, the delicious hard nougat candy made in a nearby town. My father made a long collapsible table that was set up on Uncle Pete's porch. All the young ones, numbering at least twelve, sat at that table, which would remain up until January 6.

Sleigh Bells and a Truck Full of Tree

At Christmas the women in the family made sausage, cutting the meat into very small pieces instead of grinding it, and adding wine, salt, fennel seeds, and pepper. Uncle Joe trucked in the holiday provisions. They included sacks of chestnuts, walnuts, almonds and filberts, grapes, pears, apples, tangerines, dates, prickly pears, pomegranates, fresh fennel, mushrooms, artichokes, and macaroni. Aunt Concetta had a root cellar to keep everything fresh, and a cousin owned a live poultry market, making the deliveries in a horse-drawn sleigh in the snow, often giving us kids a ride.

The last thing to come off Uncle Joe's truck was the huge tree, which was set up at the end of the porch.

Christmas Eve dinner was served late. It started with antipasto, then macaroni, then salad and the entrée. Traditionally there were twelve kinds of fish, and the dinner ended with fruits and wine. Coffee and the pastries came next, including homemade struffoli, sweet round pastries, and zeppoli, another sweet delicacy.

For the remainder of the evening we played Lotto, roulette or cards. We kids had napped earlier, so we could stay up. Uncle Rudy dressed as Santa at midnight and came from the attic with gifts.

On Christmas day the men paid calls on other relatives, and dinner started at about three p.m. Friends and relatives visited, and there would be music and singing, and games later on. It would all happen again on New Year's, with the addition of champagne at midnight. The festivities kept going until January 6 and it was usual for about fifty family members to gather at each event.

There were feasts during March, and again on Easter Sunday when we would enjoy delicious Easter Cake, a deep-dish creation with a rich custard filling. A bit later in the year, our family's celebratory traditions would begin all over again.

Chapter Two
"Look at That Little Boy
Trying to Make Music!"

MY CAREER AS A PIANIST started in 1925, when I was five years old. I was at my aunt's house, playing with her new puppy, while my cousin Iris was having a piano lesson. When Iris finished and was busy talking to her teacher, I figured it was my turn, so I went to the piano and did just what I'd watched her do. I remember to this day thinking that the sounds I was producing from that instrument were absolutely incredible and that I had no intention of stopping. I continued to pound the keys, figuring there was a tune in there somewhere.

It turns out the teacher, Professor Vincent Coppola, had been watching and was impressed, too. He turned to my cousin Iris and said, "Look at that little boy trying to make music. He's at a good age to start taking lessons."

Later that day, when my father returned from work, Iris came over to our house and repeated the teacher's remark. My father, a musician himself, was a big believer in musical education, so he wasted no time in teaching me "Solfeggio," a way of learning to sight-read and keep time with the musical notes. About two months later, my father decided I was ready to undertake piano lessons, so he and my mother went into Manhattan from our house in Brooklyn and bought a Hardman Peck upright piano. It was one of the finest instruments of its day and, at one time, the official piano of the Metropolitan Opera.

My parents knew I was very serious about practicing, and they wanted a solid piano that would stand up to it. Some days later, when the piano was delivered, I was as happy as a child is with a new toy. I took to that piano as if I had been born to it. Though I was only five years old, Professor Coppola agreed to take me on as a pupil. I amazed him by memorizing my entire first week's lessons.

Thus began my musical career.

My interest in that wonderful instrument never faltered, and soon I was Professor Coppola's prize pupil. It was almost like having another father. He was a very demanding teacher, but was pleased with how I retained all he taught me and how I progressed under his tutelage. As a result, there were many times when he stayed much beyond the one hour allotted for my lesson. Very often we spent the extra time playing duets.

Every morning at seven a.m., like clockwork, I was at the piano practicing my lessons until eight forty-five, when I would leave to go to school. As the lessons became more difficult and I needed more time to practice, I headed for the piano again after school from three p.m. until suppertime. After supper my father would sit in a chair near the piano and ask me to play whatever piece I had learned that day. Though he was generally pleased with my playing, there were times when he criticized me and exhorted me to do better.

He would say, "You need to concentrate more on those difficult passages and musical phrases until they sound good."

My mother would intercede for me, saying, "James, he did study hard today, but you know he has schoolwork and it does take some of his time away from the piano."

A Father to Be Proud Of

I would not have become a pianist without my father by my side.

My father, Vitaliano James Tramontana, was born in 1889 in Soverato, Italy. He came to America at the age of sixteen, after his own father died. Young as he was, he was alone, living in a boarding house in Lower Manhattan, working as a Bank of America teller, and attending school at night. He quickly learned English, and continued his studies at Cooper Union. Not only was his English excellent, but his handwriting was uncommonly beautiful.

Dad was of medium height, thin, fair, and fine-featured. He was always well-groomed in custom-made clothes that always fit the season; he had a quiet elegance. Every summer he would purchase black-and-white shoes and a straw hat. In winter it would be gray suede spats and matching gloves.

My father was accomplished on both guitar and mandolin, though he thought the violin a more delicate instrument, and he was determined to master it, which he eventually did. Dad started out by practicing noisily at his boarding house, until there were so many complaints from his neighbors that he had to take to the roof. One night in summer, when windows were open, somebody tied cowbells to the chimney, and pulled the ropes when Dad started to practice, creating a terrible ruckus that drowned out his violin.

That ended Dad's practicing the violin until he married and had his own apartment. Though he was self-taught, he always knew how a piece of music should sound.

Practice Was My Playtime

My days were pretty much filled, as I practiced in the morning, after school, and in the evening, and did my schoolwork in between. I had very little playtime, but I did not mind because I loved my music. Like my father's experience, my practicing wasn't universally approved though there were no cowbells.

Unfortunately my siblings, Joe and Adele, were unhappy with this arrangement because they could not listen to their favorite radio programs while I was practicing. You have to remember this was much before the advent of TV.

In 1927, about two years after I started taking piano lessons, my father thought my brother Joe should start on the violin, because violin and piano was a popular combination. Once again he started teaching "Solfeggio" and when he figured Joe was ready, he engaged a teacher for him, whether my brother liked the violin or not. Unfortunately, Joe didn't like the violin . While Joe had a good ear for music, in his teacher's estimation he was not progressing as he should.

Poor Joe! He struggled with that burden for years until my mother acknowledged that Joe's heart was just not in it. She said he should put the violin back in its case. This ended Joe's musical career. Adele decided to study the piano later in life, though she didn't go further with it. By making an effort, they both contributed to my father's dream of a musical education for each one of us.

A House Filled with Music

On Friday nights in the late 1920s, our house was filled with music. My father's friend Vito, who played the mandolin, banjo, and guitar, came over and my father, who could also play guitar, joined him. Later, a neighbor, Mr. Merryfield from upstairs, who played violin, made three. While I played piano, my mother's cousin Joe played clarinet. We all played together in one great big jam session. My mother, who had a beautiful voice and who had studied opera, chimed in, singing renditions of operatic and popular Italian and American songs. Later, two of my friends, Armand and Eugene Dryer, both accomplished violinists, joined the group.

It was a beautiful musical time. Too bad we can't bring that time back again.

Though the violin was not for Joe, he did follow his heart and became an engineer. Among his credits was his work on the Manhattan Project at Columbia University where he met Enrico Fermi, John Dunning, Harold Urey, Robert Oppenheimer, and other renowned scientists.

The Pale Little Performer at Carnegie Hall

January 1926 was a memorable time in my life. Both my father and Professor Coppola were so proud of the progress I had made in learning the piano that they entered my name in a musical competition for young children sponsored by the Italian newspaper *Il Corriere Della Serra,* with an audition to be held at Carnegie Hall. Unfortunately on the day of the competition, I was sick in bed. The weather outside was also bad; it was snowing.

My mother, concerned for my welfare, said to my father, "James! In his condition and with this weather, he cannot go. Look how pale he is. Do you want him to catch pneumonia?"

My father, though also concerned about my condition, said, "I hear what you are saying, but if he misses this chance, there might not be another one. Can't we bundle him up and take him in a taxi? In this way he won't be exposed to the weather."

Though still very much concerned, my mother reluctantly agreed. She dressed me in my new suit and even applied a light shade of rouge to my face to counteract my startling paleness. When the taxi arrived, she bundled me up with a hat, my winter coat, and a wool scarf around my face and neck. Off we went to Carnegie Hall in Manhattan.

We found the place mobbed with other contestants, their parents and friends, and other ticket holders. To say that I was nervous when I saw that most of the other contestants were much older than I is putting it mildly. I was flat out scared. We took our seats and I listened to the other contestants play their various musical instruments.

Wait Until They Hear You Play!

My father, seeing that I was a bit nervous, tried to calm me, saying, "Don't be nervous. You are going to do just fine. Wait until they hear you play!"

When they called my name, the audience was awestruck to see this little six-year-old boy climb onto the piano bench and start to play. They had expected a much older and bigger person. Boy, were they surprised! My parents and my teacher were overjoyed when I won the Silver Medal. Everyone at school and in the neighborhood congratulated me. I was the star in town. My piano teacher was especially beaming, since my success reflected so well on his teaching.

The following year, my teacher was smiling even more broadly, because I entered the contest again, and this time was awarded a Gold Medal.

As Adele wrote in the family memoir, "From then on, it was one award-winning contest after another. Dolph was a child prodigy and was in constant demand. Mom and Dad accompanied him to all his public appearances, because he was too young to travel alone."

Perfect Pitch, a Gift You Cannot Learn

Once a month Mr. Mazzanoble, a piano tuner, came to our house to tune my piano, and I sat and watched as he worked. Usually he would have a big fat cigar in his mouth as he leaned over the piano. Normally the tuner plays a triad of three notes and, using a tuning fork to set the pitch, he adjusts the tension on the strings.

One day, after he finished, I told him that some of the notes did not sound quite right. I was seven years old. Imagine my telling a veteran piano tuner that some of his tuning was off! Mr. Mazzanoble was flabbergasted.

"What makes you think some keys are not perfectly tuned?"

I replied, "Because that's how they sound to me."

"Well, let's see if you really can tell. Go stand in the corner and face the wall." He proceeded to strike various keys and I correctly named each one he struck. When he leveraged his tuning wrench in order to produce discordant tones, I was able to detect the discord readily. He was amazed, telling my mother, "This boy has perfect pitch. This is an ability you do not learn, but are born with."

A Ten-Year-Old with a Radio Show

I don't know exactly why or how, but my father knew many people, and through one of them, he arranged for me to play on radio station WJZ, and would take me on Saturdays to Starlite Park where the station broadcast took place. Although I was only ten years old, I was now performing a fifteen-minute program of music every Saturday morning beginning at eleven a.m. The announcer, referring to me as a child prodigy, introduced the music I had prepared for the program. With my mother holding the stopwatch while I practiced at home, it was my responsibility to time each selection so as not to exceed the minutes allotted to me.

"The house could burn around him," my mother would say, "and he would still be playing the piano."

In 1935 I was fifteen and had two piano teachers, Professor Coppola and Miss Celia Salmon, headmistress of the Greenwich Conservatory of Music in New York City. After hearing several of my radio programs and determining that I would be a worthwhile student and an asset to the school, she began to teach me music theory. I also studied harmony and counterpoint at the Conservatory.

My mother dressed me in the fashion of the day, and on many occasions I looked like little Lord Fauntleroy with my short pants, long stockings, jacket and shirt with a Buster Brown collar. I pretty much dressed the same way whenever I accompanied my mother as she sang

17

at one of her charity organizations. Except for the Buster Brown collar, my dress code remained much the same until I graduated from junior high school.

Playing for the Masters

While I studied at the Greenwich Conservatory, some of the other students and I would periodically be driven in a limousine to the homes of some of the school's wealthy patrons and famous sponsors, who would critique our work. One sponsor was Albert Spalding, the first American violinist to appear with the Paris Conservatory Orchestra. Fritz Kreisler was another, one of the greatest and most beloved violin masters of all time, who had himself been taught by Bruckner and Massanet.

One day Miss Salmon called me into her office and said, "We are going to be honored with a visit by a very famous celebrity, who would like to hear some of you students play." The celebrity was no less than Sergei Rachmaninoff, whose music I was busy studying and practicing. What an honor, I thought! I don't know if I'd have the courage to do this now, but I chose to play something of his own for the renowned composer, the Prelude in C# Minor, popularly known as *The Bells of Moscow*, composed when he was only nineteen. Rachmaninoff had played this piece for his own debut in 1892. It is said that he only received forty rubles in payment for this now-famous work.

When it was over, Rachmaninoff complimented me on how I played his famous work, and praised Miss Salmon too, making it clear that he thought I was a good student. His compliment was a great honor for me and for the school as well.

I continued my studies with Miss Salmon for several years, and then worked for several more with Professor Coppola.

Despite being duplicated many times, this image of Grandfather, Giuseppe Cacciaguida Pannuccio, originally an oil painting, says a great deal about his character and his upbringing.

Grandmother, Giovanna Arlotta Cacciaguida, was highly respected, an immensely popular friend to many. When she died, bouquets of flowers lined the stairs to her home.

First Name:	*Maria*
Last Name:	*Cacciaguida*
Ethnicity:	*Italy, Italian South*
Last Place of Residence:	*Italy*
Date of Arrival:	*May 11, 1904*
Age at Arrival:	*12* *Gender: F · Marital Status: S*
Ship of Travel:	*Liguria*
Port of Departure:	*Napoli*
Manifest Line Number:	*0011*

© 2001 by Intellectual Reserve, Inc. All rights reserved.

A contemporary version of my mother's entry information as she arrived in America in May, 1904, at the age of twelve.

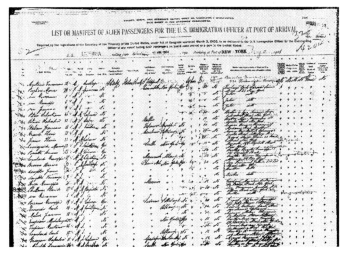

Somewhere on this official ship manifest is my mother's name. The pain of her year apart from her family and her difficult trip on the Liguria was eased by her later devotion to the family she so lovingly cared for.

My mother and father, February, 1919.
Dad was thirty, Mother twenty-seven.

My mother, Marie Tramontana, second from left, with her brothers
and sister. At her left is Anthony Cacciaguida. To her right are Peter
Cacciaguida, Nettie Ida, and John and Rudolfo Cacciaguida.

Chapter Three
My Father, No Longer by My Side

IN 1934, when I was fourteen years old, my father died. He was only forty-five years old. We were devastated.

Professor Coppola took on even more importance in my musical life at that time, becoming like a godfather to me. But my father was irreplaceable. I think the secret to his powerful support of me was that he had played the violin himself in his earlier years, when he first came to America. Without his understanding and encouragement, I might never have been given the enormous opportunities to learn the piano that I enjoyed. My father made it clear that he never regretted the decision he made to offer me lessons when he found me trying to make music on my aunt's piano.

My father always talked proudly about me. If he saw an opportunity and thought it might benefit me, he always encouraged me to try it. He was a better manager than anyone I could have had. What a tremendous loss! Fourteen is an impressionable age, a time when a boy needs the guidance of a father. His death was a tragedy to my sister, brother, and mother for emotional as well as financial reasons. Bless her soul, my mother followed my father's example after his death and continued to encourage me in all my musical endeavors. She never lost faith in me and urged me to continue my studies.

I accompanied my mother for years as she sang operatic arias and other popular songs, which proved to be great practice and a very good thing, enabling me to easily accompany countless singers and musicians in every category during my later years. I developed a special feel for these performers and found myself able to trust my judgment about how a given work should be performed. Eventually, I earned a reputation as a fine accompanist, a reputation I'm truly proud of, one that has taken me all over the world.

A Tough Piano to Move

The Hardman Peck piano my father and mother had bought for me was especially well-made, so it was heavy. We moved a few times after my father died, and always had to call the Santini Brothers, who knew how to move pianos. A block and tackle would have to be attached to the roof in order to lift the piano up through the window. During one move the company did that, as usual, but the hoists did not hold, and the parapet, weakened by the first move, gave way altogether.

The ropes came loose and the piano slid, but luckily did not slam into the building. Fortunately, the workman who guided the piano and saved it from destruction was not hurt. Within two years we moved again, and this time the movers were prepared and everything went well. On the following move, however, the stairs could not take the piano's weight, so hoisting it via the roof was the only answer. But it would not fit through the window.

The men wanted to remove the window casing, but the landlord said no. The piano remained hovering in midair while discussions went on, and we were aware that movers get paid by the hour. Mom was convinced the piano would come crashing down and kill someone. The landlord was adamant, but allowed me to practice on the first floor, where he also had a piano. Mama very reluctantly agreed, and the men lowered the piano and put it back in the truck.

Seeing the truck leave with our piano still on it was a bleak moment for all of us as we remembered much happier times when my father was still with us. The Santini men carried that piano with them from job to job until, after a few days of my practicing in his house, the landlord relented. You can try again, he said, if Mom will be responsible for any damage to the roof, and if she would agree to pay for the

26

removal of the window and any damage.

Mom was so unnerved by all this that she swore we would never move again unless the move was to our own house.

My First Pair of Long Pants

We had a tough time at home financially after my dad passed away. One of my mother's solutions was to approach Professor Coppola, asking him if he would teach me to play popular music so that perhaps I could earn some money to help the family. Unfortunately, Professor Coppola was trained to teach only classical music and was not versed in the popular music of the '20s and '30s. The poor man understood our situation, and felt bad that he could offer no help. My mother had run out of Dad's insurance money and indicated to Professor Coppola that, though my lesson cost only three dollars per week, I would have to stop them. The professor was not happy to hear this, and said, "He should not stop studying no matter what, even if you can't pay me."

In a later conversation with her older brother, Peter, my mother let slip that she was stopping my piano lessons. My uncle was an undertaker and fairly well fixed financially. He told my mother, "No, Elsie. Don't stop his lessons. I'll pay for them and whatever else he needs. He is my godson."

That's how I was able to continue with my studies.

I was in the orchestra while I attended Seth Low Junior High and was asked to lead the orchestra for graduation. I had written the school song and they wanted me to play it. I believe the song is still being played. For this occasion, Mama bought me my first pair of long pants—white flannels, with a blue jacket and black-and-white shoes.

Though my father would never have allowed me to play the popular tunes of the day, while in high school in 1935, I joined a small group that played popular music for school functions. I also played in a local beer garden. Once my orchestra and I played a wedding for some people associated with the White Rose food company. That night, in addition to our pay of three dollars each, we were given cans of food to take home.

As luck would have it, one of the boys said he had gotten a job at a hotel in the Catskill Mountains and would like me to join the group as their piano player. Apart from the fact that I was a good musician who could play all kinds of music, they felt I was also a good accompanist, having accompanied my mother for all those years. Various performers were expected to appear and they needed an all-around accompanist.

The Big Job at Ten Dollars a Week

I was very excited. I now had a summer job that was going to pay me ten dollars a week! Though she needed the money I would send her, my mother wasn't so excited and told me not to go to the Catskills— one, because I was only sixteen, two, because I'd have to quit my piano lessons, and three, because I'd be in a strange place with strangers. Some of my uncles and aunts overheard these arguments and interceded with me until my mother agreed, provided I promised I would still practice my lessons.

This was the start of my jazz career, which was known at the time as Pop music. It was also the first holiday away from home and my family that I had as a youngster, and it proved to be a wonderful summer. At many of the hotels I worked, the guests were amazed at how often they would see me practice. They did not understand that, because I was away from my teachers and lessons, I had no choice but to keep learning on my own. I practiced several hours each morning, and then in the afternoon I rehearsed for the show. The performers took a liking to me because of the way I accompanied them, and many were amazed at my ability. After rehearsals I went swimming or engaged in sports. I missed my family and wrote a letter home every week.

That summer in the Catskills I realized I would be spending a good part of my life away from home and this was how my life was always going to be.

Since this was my first time away from home, my mother worried about me, as all mothers do. She wondered if I ate enough proper food, got enough rest, and all the other things mothers worry about. My brother and sister also missed me, but in a way they were glad I was not there, because they could finally hear their favorite radio programs without my constant need to practice in the same room with the radio.

"No, I'm Not Jewish," I said in Yiddish.

Although I am not Jewish, the owners of the hotels I worked for treated me as one of their family. One day one of the guests in a certain hotel approached me and asked, "Where is your yarmulka?" When he learned that I was not Jewish, he became upset and berated the hotel owner for hiring a goy. What he didn't know is that I grew up in an Italian-Jewish neighborhood, so I answered the guest in Yiddish. Boy, was he surprised! The owner told him he liked my work so much, in fact, that I was the sole reason he was keeping the band on. After the guest calmed down and he and his wife listened to my playing, they became two of my most ardent supporters.

When summer was over, those same boys and I formed our own band and played at many small functions and parties. As a result, I was now earning some money and could help defray household expenses and the cost of my lessons with Professor Coppola. He was amazed at how much I was earning, but was a bit unhappy as well, since he felt playing jazz was seriously interrupting my classical studies.

I started to work with larger orchestras and even did some arranging for several of the orchestras I played with. Soon I gained a reputation as a fine arranger and accompanist and started to work with minor celebrities on their way up to fame, including Frank Sinatra, whom I first worked with in a group called "The Brooklyn Boys."

Among the others I worked with were Tony Bennett (whose real name was Anthony Di Benedetto), Vic Damone, Georgia Gibbs, Rosie Clooney, and so on. There were many others as well, all talented performers.

The Welcome Birth of the Big Bands

When I was seventeen, Buddy Katz, one of my longtime high school friends, asked me to go with him to meet Jerry Blaine, an up-and-coming bandleader. Blaine had big eyes and a moon face, and was a genuinely nice guy who would later establish Jubilee Records, but right now he needed a pianist. Because my prospects were otherwise dim at that time, I thought why not? I joined a rehearsal, where I met many of Blaine's musicians. After hearing me play, Jerry offered me a job, and soon we left for the Deschler Wallick Hotel in Columbus, Ohio playing in several theaters in Ohio as well. We did a theater tour with Lucille Ball and a young girl named Mia Farrow, who was traveling with her mother, the famous actress Maureen O'Sullivan.

I eventually left Jerry Blaine's band because of dissension among several musicians. A couple of the boys were practical jokers. One of them stuffed rags deep into the bell of a band member's trombone, so that when the trombonist tried to play, there was no sound. The trombonist extracted the rags with some difficulty, and was incensed. Some of the boys thought it was funny, but the trombonist did not. Some weeks later he, too, quit the band.

That guy never quite got over that incident. Every time I'd see him, he'd say, "Hey, remember what they did to my trombone?"

It wouldn't be long before I'd find out what it's like to work with serious musicians, the finest talent in the nation.

Age nine, doing what I love best, then and now.

With Buddy Katz, Dobby Dobson and an unidentified singer, performing for Uncle Sam on Staten Island during the 1940s.

Our six-piece 1944 Army Band with Benny Caruso, Nat Cohen, Nick Perito, Buddy Katz, and Eddie Aversano.

There was nothing fancy about Army Band rehearsals,
especially in the warm weather.

Playing piano for one of the very earliest television shows ever
broadcast. This was at Dumont Broadcasting, and must be
Army-related, since I'm in uniform.

No longer in uniform, here I am with my friend the singer Jerry
Baker at Oetjen's Restaurant in Brooklyn, 1946. Jerry had an
enormously popular radio show at the time on WMCA.
While you were waiting for Jack Benny, Superman
and Tom Mix, you listened to Jerry.

Conducting the Army Band in 1944 on Staten Island.

Chapter Four
Our Big Band and Its Skinny Little Singer

IN 1935, Benny Goodman hosted a weekly Saturday-night radio show that was on the air from coast to coast. For the first time, all of America could hear a truly outstanding swing band. People needed hope, and the Big Bands gave it to them.

In 1939, Harry James left Benny Goodman's band, where he was the star soloist, to start a band of his own, bankrolled by Goodman himself. Harry needed a piano player for this new band, known as Harry James and His Orchestra. He asked his musicians for recommendations and they suggested me. Harry asked me to join his seventeen-piece orchestra when I was only nineteen.

Harry James was only twenty years old when he was given the chance to join Benny Goodman. Maybe that's the reason Harry didn't think I was too young when he hired me. And after all, he was only twenty-three. Looking at early photos of these guys, we realize that people grew up faster in those days. Though Tommy Dorsey looked (and acted) like a suave battlefield general, he too was only a kid.

Harry was a tall, thin guy with a high, squeaky voice and a Texas accent. He was in love with his trumpet, the Brooklyn Dodgers, and (later) Betty Grable. Like me, he had gotten an early start, encouraged by a father who expected him to practice for hours every day, and to consider perfecting his musicianship his first priority.

Most people don't know that Harry James was the son of circus performers. His father was a circus bandleader and horn-player and his mother ("The Iron Jaw") an aerialist who hung suspended from a wire by her teeth. Harry himself had worked the circus as soon as he

35

could walk.

Harry was three when he played the drums for circus audiences and five when he performed as a contortionist known as "The Human Eel." He was eight when he started playing the trumpet and twelve when he took over conducting the circus's second band, which schooled him to play loud, hard blues. This intense early training was probably why he had been nicknamed "The Hawk" when he was playing with Benny Goodman, for his uncanny ability to sight-read; musicians used to joke that if a fly landed on his music score, Harry would play it.

From the very first bar, radio audiences knew immediately that it was Harry James at the microphone. His low range had a warmth associated with the cornet and even the flugelhorn, not often heard on the trumpet, a sound beautifully offset by his brilliant high register. The great *San Francisco Chronicle* columnist Herb Caen remembered "Harry James puffing out his cheeks till surely they must burst, the rhythm always burning and churning and driving you out of your mind."

I Join a Dream Team

I was ecstatic when Harry asked me to join his fantastic group. Not only was he already one of America's great instrumentalists and an outstanding soloist, master of the bravura trumpet, he was well-liked and respected in the business. That was important to me. Harry James was the 1930s equivalent of a rock star. He put together only top-notch musicians for his first trip out on his own, and I was very happy in his band.

At one point there were 400 big bands ranging in style from strong swing to sweet. America was counting on us to help it forget its wartime troubles, and we were glad to oblige.

We individual musicians played a big role in the success of the Harry James band. It was well known that the attitudes and sense of cooperation among musicians could make or break a band. We all got along well with each other and supported Harry fully, which showed in the music. While Glenn Miller, Benny Goodman, Artie Shaw, and Tommy Dorsey were known for putting the pressure on, leaning heavily on their musicians to get what they wanted, Harry was equally devoted to high musical standards, but his way of getting perfection was much more relaxed.

Harry's way of getting what he wanted was to hire the best talent, and then leave it up to us to produce at the highest level.

When the musical history of this wonderful era came to be written years later, it was commonly acknowledged that the morale of the individual musicians was generally highest in the bands that played the best music and were headed by leaders who knew how to treat the men respectfully. The leaders always singled out as good examples of this attitude are Les Brown, Woody Herman, Duke Ellington, Count Basie, the other Dorsey—Jimmy— and of course my boss, Harry James.

A Magic Voice from the Rustic Cabin

The Harry James Band was easy to listen to and great to dance to. It's hard to convey to younger people today exactly how devoted to us our audiences were. Big Bands are often compared with major league sports teams when it comes to describing the fever pitch of devotion our fans would reach. Later, the decibel level created by audiences screaming for a certain skinny singer would illustrate that better than any description I could offer.

When I joined his band in 1939, Harry's vocalist was twenty-four-year-old Frank Sinatra. He was a lightweight to all appearances but that's where it ended.

Singer Louise Tobin, Harry's wife at the time, would tell how she discovered Frank. It seems Harry was napping one day and Louise, who was about to leave for a gig with Buddy Hackett's band in Boston, heard Frank sing on the radio from the Rustic Cabin in Englewood, New Jersey, where he was also a waiter. She wasn't blown away or anything. She thought Frank was a fair singer, not great, but thought that maybe, somehow, this unknown young guy would be able to give Harry what he needed at the microphone for a while.

Louise woke Harry up. He turned up the radio, listened, and agreed.

In June, 1939, the famous Harry James strode into the Rustic Cabin, delighting the owner, Harry Nichols. How about that boy singer he heard on the radio? Harry asked Nichols. "We don't have a singer," was the reply. "We just have an emcee who sings a little bit." Just then, a skinny waiter took off his apron and climbed the stage.

Years later, Harry remembered, "He'd sung only eight bars when I felt the hairs on the back of my neck rising. I knew he was destined to be a great vocalist."

Harry asked Frank to meet him at the Paramount Theatre where they signed a deal. Harry's band was only three months old. On June 30 we played a weeklong engagement at the Hippodrome in Baltimore. Frank was so new to the band, he wasn't even listed on the bill.

Soon the screaming started in the theater, and girls were lining up backstage.

I was receiving $300 per week working for Harry James, while there was a rumor that Frank only got $15. Actually, Harry offered him $75.

Frank was apparently used to being underpaid. He once wrote the foreword to a book about the Big Bands, and in it he said, "Working with a good band in those days was the end of the rainbow for any singer who wanted to make it in this profession. [Before joining Harry James] I had been in a panic period, I was on four local stations, and I planned it so I'd be on the air every three hours all through the day. Don't think I was doing all this work for nothing—I got seventy cents carfare from Jersey to the Mutual Studios [where WOR broadcast, in New York City]."

Full of Zip, Zap, and Zing

It was always Louise Tobin's opinion that Frank learned more, musically, in his short time with our band than he'd previously learned in his life. Frank loved James's hot, sentimental music. It was the sound that taught him how to load his song with emotion, taking him to a level far beyond the abilities of his earliest hero, Bing Crosby.

Harry James would later say that he considered Sinatra a very serious singer, from the very beginning of their working together. There was no kidding with Frank about his music, Harry said. When Frank sang, *he sang.*

In the commentary to his own *Man and His Music* album in 1965, Frank remembered his early days with us: "I was young and full of zip, zap, and zing, and I was also full of myself." Maybe so, but nobody worked harder than that young man to perfect his signature "effortless" sound.

I know. I was there.

Frank always called Harry James "Boss" when he was singing with us and he continued to call him that for the rest of his life. He considered Harry a dear friend and great teacher.

Working with Harry James's top-notch Big Band was as satisfying for me as it was for Frank, despite some of the touring conditions we shared. Gene Krupa once compared the traveling experiences of ballplayers and musicians, saying they were almost identical.

> The road, the living out of suitcases, the constant time pressures to get to another place so that you can perform on schedule, the working with the same people every day, being watched all the time by the public, trying to live up to a reputation, and, of course, all the mental and emotional intangibles that must affect ballplayers just the way they affect musicians.

I might as well let Frank Sinatra add to that description of the life we both lived. In that same foreword, he wrote:

When it comes to professional experience, there's nothing to beat those one-nighter tours, when you rotate between five places around the clock—the bus, your hotel room, the greasy-spoon restaurant, the dressing room (if any) and the bandstand. Then back on the bus to the next night's gig, maybe 400 miles away or more.

Frank neglected to mention all of the out-of-tune pianos, stages that were too small, and bad sound systems we endured along the way.

It turns out that Tommy Dorsey had his eye on Frank, whom he called "that skinny kid with James," since Jack Leonard, Dorsey's popular vocalist, had been drafted into the Army. Jack was also eager to get out from under Tommy's strong control.

When we were working at the Sherman Hotel in Chicago in late 1939, Tommy sent an emissary to see if Frank was interested in taking Leonard's place, predicting Frank would become as big as Crosby. Naturally, Frank was excited. He went to Harry James and explained that Tommy had offered him Jack Leonard's spot.

Tommy Gets the Mob's Message

Harry was a great guy, and he realized that going with Tommy would be a better opportunity for Frank, especially since Nancy Sinatra was pregnant at the time. So Harry released Frank from his contract.

We played our last performance with Frank in Buffalo at Shea's Theater. Many years later Frank told an interviewer how he felt that night.

The bus pulled out with about half the boys at half-past midnight. I'd said goodbye to them all and it was snowing. There was nobody around, and I stood alone in the snow with just my suitcase and watched the taillights disappear. Then the tears started, and I tried to run after the bus. There was such spirit and enthusiasm in that band.

I hated leaving it.

A few days later, in Milwaukee, Frank joined the Tommy Dorsey Band. Friends reported that he would miss us for the next five months.

In his new spot, Frank's popularity skyrocketed. He spent three years with Dorsey and then, always interested in improving his situation, he received an offer to appear at the New York Paramount Theatre. Frank asked Tommy to release him from his contract so he could go out on his own.

Tommy was not a nice person and refused to release Frank. Frank mentioned his dilemma to a well-placed friend, reputed to be one of the top Mob bosses. The Mob boss made it known to Tommy that if he did not release Frank from his contract, the Mob would see to it that the Dorsey band would never receive engagements in any big hotels or nightclubs or on any major broadcasts.

I guess Tommy believed the Mob boss, because he reluctantly released Frank, in exchange for $75,000.

Sinatra Holds on to His Good Name

The Big Band era lasted from the mid-1930s to the mid-1940s. It's a source of pride to me that the Harry James Band remains, to this day, one of the most distinguished bands in American history. As luck would have it, my tenure coincided with the band's most successful time. George Simon (Carly's father) gave Frank his first review, in *Metronome*, when Frank was one of us in the James band. It wasn't such a hot review, either, something about Frank's "pleasing vocals," but it was extremely important to Frank, and opened many doors for him.

One Sinatra biographer said about our band at the time: "The singer was a genius, the trumpeter-leader a kind of genius. The band was terrific, and light-years from the rinky-dink six-piece outfit at the Rustic Cabin."

Another writer described the heyday of Big Bands such as ours: "Those early days when the band had such tremendous spirit, when it was filled with laughs and good humor and ambition and a healthy desire to play and swing and succeed." Here's how the influential *Metronome* magazine described us: "Harry James has the greatest white band in the country, and, for that matter... the greatest dance band ever known. And that's leaving out nobody!"

Given a start like that, it's not surprising that Harry would go on conducting a band in his own name for forty years.

Harry always knew what he had in Frank Sinatra, and was proud of the fact that his Big Band was the first to feature him.

An Affront to a Proud Family

But there was one thing Harry James wanted from Frank that I'm glad he didn't get. Harry was fresh from changing his girl singer's name from Yvonne Marie Antoinette JaMai to Connie Haines—because it rhymed with "James"— and wanted to do the same for Frank. "But," argued Frank, "I've got a cousin in New England with a band, and his name is Ray Sinatra, and he's doing fine." Frank had had earlier experience with using a name change—"Frankie Trent"—and was disgusted with himself for doing that. Besides, his mother, the fiery Dolly, gave him hell when she heard about what Harry wanted.

There was another deep-seated reason behind Frank's refusal. His father, Marty, a boxer, was forced to change his ring name to "Marty O'Brien" because an Italian name would have barred him from training gyms. That was a painful fact in a proud family, and Frank didn't want it repeated.

Connie Haines, by then an old lady, clearly remembered the moment when Frank said a final no to Harry. She said Frank's blue eyes went cold, as he said to Harry, "You want the singer, take the name."

A good thing, too. Because the name Harry James chose for his star singer was even worse than "Frankie Trent." This name would have been a great one… for a Vegas Lounge Lizard. If he had agreed with the Boss, Frank Sinatra would have spent the rest of his life behind a microphone as… "Frankie Satin."

Sometimes it pays to be pigheaded.

Somewhere in Texas, with Buddy Katz, Russ Gary,
Tommy Dale, Jimmy Patti, Teddy Stevens and
Herbie "Dobby" Dobbson.

Chuck Catania, Teddy Stevens and I at the Park Plaza Hotel in St.
Louis. Teddy was the father of my godchild Connie Stevens.

Audrey, 1961. The pianist always played "The Most Beautiful Girl in the World" as Audrey walked the runway at the Waldorf, modeling for high-fashion houses. And he was right.

"Appearing Nightly, Dolph Traymon, His Piano and His Orchestra." A 1950s Atlantic City Visitors' Guide ad for the Hotel Senator's Sun & Star Roof.

Elissa (at piano) and Tracey

Audrey's wonderful mother, Florence Wrench, with whom we happily shared a home at different times. We got along great, but family legend has it that when I got out of hand, Florence would straighten me out by starching my boxer shorts.

Chapter Five
A "Bravo!" from Maestro Toscanini

IN 1940, one of my neighbors in the Bensonhurst section of Brooklyn was Umberto Penino, who played first trumpet with the NBC Symphony Orchestra, which was heard by millions on radio daily. One day Umberto invited me to attend a rehearsal at Carnegie Hall, promising he would introduce me to the conductor.

This was no ordinary conductor. It was the world-renowned Arturo Toscanini, one of the most acclaimed musicians in two centuries and without a doubt the greatest conductor of the twentieth. Toscanini's 1936 recording of Beethoven's *Seventh Symphony* with the New York Philharmonic is still regarded as one of the greatest recordings of all time.

After defying both Hitler and Mussolini, Toscanini refused to return to his beloved Italy while it was in the hands of the Fascists, so the famous orchestra he would be rehearsing was created and trained especially for him.

Toscanini was noted for his perfectionism, his impeccable musical ear, his intensity, his photographic memory... and his world-class temper. His ferocious temper was so famous that it was spoofed in Tom and Jerry cartoons.

Toscanini was also well-known for not allowing spectators to attend his rehearsals! Would I get to see that terrible temper in person? And, would it be directed at me?

Playing Ludwig for Arturo

It turned out that my friend Umberto had not invited me as a spectator, however. After the rehearsal, which I remember was a symphony, he retrieved me from the audience to take me to meet Toscanini. I was surprised that the great man was short in stature, about five-feet-five, but not surprised that he was a dynamic personality.

"Dolph is a budding classical pianist," Umberto told Toscanini, who proceeded to speak to me in Italian, asking me where and with whom I studied. While I could understand some Italian, I could not carry on a long conversation in it, so I was relieved when he switched to English.

Then something happened that I could never have imagined or even wished for.

Could it be possible that Arturo Toscanini is asking me to play a Beethoven Sonata for him? Right now?

My God, this was the genius who revolutionized musical interpretation by insisting that scores be played exactly as written, a highly unusual practice in the nineteenth century when Toscanini began his career. This is a man who knew Verdi personally; who conducted the world premieres of Puccini's *La Boheme, Turandot,* and *Pagliacci.*

And it was me and Beethoven he was waiting to hear.

There was no decision-making time possible, no opportunity for hesitation.

I sat down at the orchestra's piano and played a piece I knew well, Beethoven's *Moonlight Sonata.*

The Applause That Changed My Life

I finished the sonata and took a breath. I was pleased, but how would my important audience react?

The sound of Arturo Toscanini applauding enthusiastically for me is a sound I'll never forget. On top of it, he was crying "Bravo."

I was thrilled. That wasn't all. Some members of the NBC Orchestra had stayed to listen and joined the Maestro in his applause.

I was jubilant. What a dream come true!

Then it got even better.

Toscanini asked me if I had ever heard of the Juilliard School of Music. I replied that yes, I had heard of it, but had never thought of studying there because my family could not afford it.

The Maestro thought about this for a few minutes, and then asked, "Would you be willing to audition for a scholarship?"

"Of course!" I replied. "Yes!"

"Let me see if I can arrange something," said the Maestro.

A key to Toscanini's willingness to seek out and take seriously a young, unknown but promising musician may lay in the fact that as a child he had benefited from such an intervention himself. At the age of nine, in the second grade at his school in Parma, one of young Arturo's teachers recognized him as a prodigy and urged his parents to enroll him at the royal conservatory.

Luckily, Toscanini's parents did what the teacher suggested. The result was the genius who would later make his conducting debut with *Aida* at the age of nineteen in Rio de Janeiro. *Aida* was one of 160 operas he would conduct from memory.

Good News from Juilliard

Several days after performing for Toscanini, I received a letter in the mail from the Juilliard School of Music, saying that an audition had been set up for me.

This was my big chance. I chose several of the most difficult musical pieces that I had learned under Professor Coppola, and practiced them like mad.

I played Felix Mendelssohn's romantic Rondo Capriccioso, op.14, which some say he wrote as early as the age of eighteen. Then I played two of the most technically demanding pieces in the piano literature, selected from Franz Lizst's *Grande Etudes,* a tribute to the exquisite violin work of Paganini. The two etudes I played were La Campanella, Etude 3, which requires quiet playing with a mystical quality, and La Chasse (*The Hunt*) Etude 5, categorized as a caprice, which well describes its impulsive, unpredictable quality. I also played Beethoven's Piano Sonata No. 8 in C Minor, op. 13, known as the *Sonata Pathetique,* with its three distinctive movements, written when Beethoven was only six years older than I was at that time.

The day arrived for my audition, and I felt fully prepared to play those and any others Juilliard might ask for.

When I arrived at the school, which was then located at 12th Street and Fifth Avenue, I was disappointed that it didn't look like the Palace of Music I had imagined. Instead, it was just a light-colored, three-story nondescript building.

I went in and presented my letter to the woman walking toward me. "Come with me," she said, and led me to a room down a hallway, a fairly large one with windows along one wall. At the far end was a grand piano. Several people were gathered off to one side, talking among themselves.

The woman brought me to the group and introduced me. One of them asked where I had studied, and with whom, and then someone asked what selections I had chosen to play. Then we got down to business.

As I walked over to the piano, the group sat in chairs placed so that they could easily observe me.

I played by memory several of the selections I had chosen. Then, before I could continue, one of the group said, ""Now we'll tell you what to play next."

And they did, while I was thinking to myself, "This is going to be a tough bunch. Well, I'll give it my best shot and let the chips fall where they may."

I played the pieces they named. When they had heard enough, I walked over, graciously thanked them for allowing me to play for them, and left.

"Well, how did you do?" my mother asked as soon as I got home. "I don't know," I said. "I played everything they asked me to play, but no one said anything."

"That's strange," she said. "You'd think someone would have said something."

"Well, I thought so too," I said. "But they were a tight-lipped bunch. I guess we'll have to wait till later to hear what they think."

By the end of that week, Juilliard had replied, and it was a yes. I was granted a scholarship. Mine was a happy house that day.

My time with Harry James was over. Hard work was ahead, and so were great musical adventures.

Juilliard and All That Jazz

At Juilliard I was fortunate to study with the great Wanda Landowska, who became world famous for her mastery of the harpsichord, introducing it to America. My fellow students and I were all very serious students, but we still had time for fun. I made many friends at Juilliard, a great bunch of talented musicians, and we had a wonderful time playing together, especially playing the things that were definitely not part of our curriculum. Ferrante and Teicher, the very popular piano duo, met at Juilliard during my years there.

When we had time off, some of us would go down to one of the basement rooms, where there was an old upright piano, to hold jam sessions for several hours. Of course, this was a novelty for some of my friends since, unlike me, none had ever played in a real jazz band.

Among my friends who took part in our jam sessions were Nanette Fabray, who later became a Broadway star, and Eddie Manson, even then a harmonica virtuoso. He and I were also both studying arranging and learning to play the clarinet.

One day Dean Wedge was escorting some guests around to see the school and became furious when he heard what we were playing. The next day we were told to report to his office, where he berated us, in no uncertain terms, for wasting our time with such junk, saying that what he overheard was not appropriate music for such a prestigious school, and that he wanted our jam sessions ended.

When I applied, Juilliard had found me so musically advanced that they thought I'd be able to graduate in only two years. But the Army thought my time at Juilliard should be cut even shorter.

Earlier, when the war began, I had been thinking that if I were ever inducted into the Army, I could probably join a marching band.

Little did I know.

A very happy November 21, 1949 at the St. Regis Maisonette after our wedding at the Mineola Courthouse. Left is Harry Pisapia, who arranged for Judge Lowell to marry us. At right is Audrey's best friend, Eleanor Schmidt, in her mother's mink stole.

1953, the eight-piece Dolph Traymon Band plays at the St. Anthony Hotel in San Antonio, Texas.

Playing in an Oyster Bay, New York radio station, WKBS, in the early 1950s.

Our five-piece band playing somewhere in Texas in the early 1950s, joined onstage by some unlucky varmints.

An illustration from an Esquire magazine piece written about the
Dolph Traymon Trio. With Russ Hale and Teddy Stevens.

Howard Tavin, Joe Sinecure and I at the Chase Hotel in St. Louis,
1944. One of our St. Louis fans, a bookie, wanted to take Audrey and
me partying at the hot spots in East St. Louis one night. But we had
no one to watch little Elissa, so the bookie said he'd send a babysitter.
That night we opened the door to a lug in a fedora chomping on a
cigar, growling, "Where's the kid?" We stayed in that night.

Chapter Six
The Pianist Plays the Pick and Shovel

THINGS WERE HEATING UP all over the world during 1941. We at home had been able to live without too much disruption—but not for long.

On the bright side, we were introduced to many things that would turn out to be American classics during that amazing year: Cheerios, Bugs Bunny, Dumbo, the Jeep, the completion of Mount Rushmore, *Citizen Kane*, Bob Hope, the USO, and Joe DiMaggio's fifty-six-game hitting streak. Life went on overseas too, sort of. Despite the blitz, a Scottish scientist discovered penicillin, and the first automatic computer was introduced in war-torn Germany.

Then the Luftwaffe bombed London's House of Commons and the Siege of Leningrad blazed in our local headlines. Greek citizens tore down the swastika from the Acropolis. The yellow Star of David first made itself known to a horrified world. The world of art and music was powerless in the face of Nazism—except for the intrepid Brecht and Weill. Their brilliant show of resistance was *Mother Courage*, even if it had to be premiered safely in neutral Zurich.

Here at home, we were hearing the terms the Air Force, the United Nations, and Defense Bonds for the first time. In New York, we knew things were getting serious when Mayor La Guardia set up Civil Air Patrols.

A few days later, on December 6, Japan changed everything by bombing Pearl Harbor. Immediately, consulates were closed on our soil, foreign ships impounded. We were at war with Germany and Japan for real.

Japan was calling up a million men, and we had to do the same.

Our country, having declared war on Germany and Japan, was drafting all boys my age, and I was no exception. On January 1, 1942, I received notice to report to an induction center, from which I was shipped to Camp Upton in Yaphank, Long Island, for basic training.

The camp had been very active during World War I and now was once again teeming with men and machines. The army didn't know it, but they were sending me to a camp with a distinguished musical history.

During WWI, one of the inductees at Camp Upton was Sergeant Irving Berlin. There he wrote one of the greatest army songs ever written and one of the all-time Berlin favorites, "Oh How I Hate to Get Up in the Morning." The song was part of a military musical he wrote called *Yip, Yip Yaphank*, based on his life at the camp, later produced on Broadway, with Berlin's fellow soldiers taking roles as cast members. In 1943 it was turned into a movie, *This Is the Army*, starring Ronald Reagan.

My Own Captain Queeg

But it would be a while before I would be returning to my own music.

Having no mechanical skills, I was assigned to a group doing general ground and maintenance duty. The sergeant in charge of our platoon was a mean individual, a source of terror to all of us young soldiers. We could do nothing about him and had no recourse. We were no longer civilians. The only thing we could do was, as the saying goes, grin and bear it.

I knew I was definitely in the army when, hearing that I was a musician, the sergeant followed traditional army logic by assigning me to pick-and-shovel duty. It became clear that he thought I was what they called an "eight ball," a guy headed for trouble, as well as a "gold-bricker" who was looking for ways to goof off.

So there I was digging ditches, breaking rocks, and practicing firing a rifle in an attempt to settle a war I did not start. It was not exactly the kind of activity a pianist's hands need. I was slamming stones instead of striking keys, feeling more and more that the years I had spent studying at home with Professor Coppola and at the Juilliard School of Music were being wasted.

Playing the Pain Away

At the end of my day's training chores, and whenever I had free time, I would go over to the Red Cross building on the post to try to get in some practicing, in spite of the fact that my hands were raw and hurting. They had an old beat-up piano that was badly in need of tuning, but I didn't care, because it allowed me to practice and somewhat keep up on my studies.

I remained at Camp Upton for six months, and then was transferred out, supposedly to be sent overseas to Europe. At the last minute, however, someone discovered that the army was short of medics. I was transferred to Halloran General Hospital on Staten Island, New York, where I was to be trained as a material medic, one who doesn't deal with dispensing medicine, but who performs other aspects of the job. With more than 3,000 beds, often jammed into small spaces, Halloran was the nation's largest Army hospital.

My duties were to help treat wounded soldiers who arrived from the battlefield with a wide range of injuries. We not only took care of soldiers returning from overseas, but also prisoners of war who were being sent back to Africa. My new duties entailed driving an ambulance back and forth from the hospital to the hospital ship to pick up the wounded. In the winter it was so cold that I placed cardboard sheets in front of the radiator to coax heat back into the vehicle's cab in an effort to keep me and my wounded passengers warm. I drove that ambulance back and forth between the hospital and ships for several months.

Finally, a Break

One day, as I was walking on the campgrounds, I happened to run into an officer, Lieutenant Herb Merin. He was an old musician friend, a drummer I had worked with some years before in one of New York's nightclubs. He recognized me, and asked, "What are you doing here?"

"I am a medic," I said. "I drive one of the ambulances."

"Has the commanding officer heard you play?"

"No, I've been here only a few months for training."

Herb said, "Meet me here tomorrow at three p.m. and we'll go to the officers' club. I want the colonel to listen to you."

The next day at the officers' club, I played for at least two hours, filling all the requests that the commanding officer, Colonel DeVoe, wanted to hear. He loved classical music—Chopin, Beethoven, and so on. The other officers were a bit annoyed, though, since they wanted me to play jazz. When I finished playing, the colonel asked me if I could organize an orchestra.

I said, "Sir, I came here from Camp Upton with several good musicians, so that will be no problem."

The Colonel said, "I will issue orders, then, to have the musicians report to you."

We started with six musicians, and as other musicians arrived in camp, they were sent to me. When any of my musician friends called me, I asked them to give me their serial numbers and had them transferred to my unit. In a short space of time, I had forty-seven musicians under my control.

We Become the Army's Star Attraction

About four months later, Colonel DeVoe sent word that sports reporter Stan Lomax, whose distinctive voice was heard for many years on New York radio station WOR, and Barry Gray from WMCA were coming to audition our orchestra for a radio show. Gray was gaining a reputation as the Father of Talk Radio. He was as important a figure as Larry King at one time, broadcasting from the Copacabana and other hot spots. Lomax and Gray were in the process of creating a show for WOR. To prepare for this audition, I scored several arrangements for my orchestra, working as hard as if we were going to play the Paramount Theatre on Broadway.

It paid off.

Lomax and Gray chose us to be their orchestra.

By this time we had grown to fifty-seven musicians. Eventually we accompanied all the top celebrities who appeared on the program, including Milton Berle, Ed Sullivan, Bob Hope, and his crew of performers.

It's fair to say that our orchestra—we never really had a name—became the army's star attraction. I conducted the orchestra for three-and-a-half-years, traveling to many states with it, raising money on War Bond and USO tours at various bases.

As a result of the orchestra's success, the two officers who headed our service unit were promoted in rank. One became a lieutenant colonel and the other a general. Our success didn't affect my rank because I was in the regular army.

Peace at Last. Now Can I Go Home?

1945. The war in Europe was over, the free world rejoiced, and it was clearly time for me to be discharged from the service.

Well, no, not so fast. Sometimes you pay a price for being a favorite. Nobody wants to let you go. That was the case with Colonel DeVoe, now General DeVoe, who wanted my band and me to stay on to play parades and other occasions for him. Actually, it was a band when it included classic band instruments, and it was an orchestra when we added, say, violins.

When I told General DeVoe that it was time for me to get back to my musical career, his answer was to offer to send me to officers' school, explaining that it would equip me to take a major position in the unit.

In other words, I could remain in the service as a sergeant major, leading the Army orchestra or bands. The problem was that as an officer, I wouldn't be allowed to play piano!

No, it was time for me to go home. I had done my duty and served my country. Now I had to concentrate on picking up my own musical career where I left off.

I continued to fulfill my musical duties, wondering when I'd be a civilian again. As luck would have it, while conducting one performance I met a colonel whose responsibility was to arrange the discharge of soldiers. I put in a phone call to him and stated my case, that, having put in three-and-a-half years in the service, I now wanted to go home.

The colonel said, "Wait a couple of weeks, and if General DeVoe doesn't release you, I'll make arrangements with him to have you discharged."

I waited several weeks and, hearing nothing about my discharge, I called him again. Three weeks later, along with several of my Army buddies, I received that long-awaited discharge.

Meanwhile, our general, who had been promoted with a second star, was unhappy to find out I had been finally discharged. When he called to tell me so, he and I agreed that if he would forget how he felt about my discharge, my buddies and I would return in civvies to play a dance session for him.

We were a sensation when we returned to Halloran, playing for all the officers we'd worked for earlier. A short time later, the general was transferred to Kingsbridge Hospital in the Bronx where he stayed until his retirement. Coincidentally, the general had a son who, in civilian life, had been the head surgeon at the Mayo Clinic. While I was a medic at Halloran Hospital, he operated on my eyes.

The general was a nice guy. About three months after I had been discharged, I called to ask for his help for my brother-in-law, Gabriel, who was in the US Cavalry. Gabe was a very short man who had Reynaud's disease, making it difficult for him to mount his horse and to withstand the cold weather in Maine where he was stationed. As a favor to me, the general had Gabe transferred to a unit in a warmer climate, where he remained until his discharge.

Chapter Seven
Breaking In with the Best in the Business

IN 1946 I WAS OUT OF THE ARMY and looking for the next step in my musical career. Walking along Broadway, I happened to bump into a friend, Jerry Baker, who had a small radio program, singing on New York station WMCA. We may not remember who Jerry is these days, but if you look at a newspaper listing of radio programs from 1946, the lineup that includes Jerry Baker is a list of American wartime cultural icons. Right before the Jerry Baker Show came on you would be able to hear Jack Benny, *Young Widder Brown*, Uncle Don, *Terry and the Pirates*, *Portia Faces Life*, *Superman*, *Dick Tracy*, *Captain Midnight*, and *Jack Armstrong*. After Jerry's program came *Tom Mix*.

Jerry was also appearing nightly in a restaurant in Brooklyn called Oetjen's. We chatted a while, and when I mentioned I was in the city looking for a job, he suggested I go see his boss, Milton Sheen, who was looking for a band to play at his restaurant.

Oetjen's was an upscale restaurant that had among its clientele many of the Brooklyn Dodgers, their families, and friends. I thought that was a good lead to take advantage of immediately, so I went to see Mr. Sheen that night. We talked about different things, including the type of music my band played. He asked how much money we were going to cost him, so I told him. He shook his head and indicated this was out of the question, so I thanked him for his time and left.

Several days later, I happened to meet Jerry again, and he asked me how I made out with Mr. Sheen. When I told him that he thought we were too expensive, he suggested that I go back and see Sheen again. He said, "He needs a band, and especially one with your talent."

When I went back to see Sheen, the first thing he said to me was, "Come on in, kid." That was his way of addressing me. "What can I do for you?"

"I would like to come and work for you," I said, "if we could work out a deal. I would like to be paid leaders' scale, and my boys ten dollars over scale. You know, with a band playing here nightly, your business will increase, because people like to hear music while they eat. Not only that, the chances are that many will stay on after dinner to have a few drinks and to dance. I would like a two-week option, with a two-month additional option if your customers like our band."

Sheen thought about it, and then agreed to the deal. I was delighted, and we set our starting date. Two weeks later, while I was conducting the show at Oetjen's, Mr. Sheen came to the bandstand and told me he wanted to pick up my option. I told him we could talk about it when I finished playing. When I came off the bandstand, l told him that we had just finished our two-week engagement and reminded him that in our previous conversation, he had indicated he couldn't afford my band. Mr. Sheen had to agree with me that his business had increased because of our music. He asked me how much money I wanted for an extended gig. My answer was the original amount I had asked for when we first met. He agreed, and we signed a contract for a year.

Six months later, Sheen gave me a raise. I wound up spending three years with Oetjen's and receiving raises every year. The restaurant's regulars included Leo Durocher (the legendary manager of the Dodgers), Eddie "The Brat" Stanky (major league second baseman and manager), Jackie Robinson (the famous ball player who broke baseball's color barrier), Pete Reiser (who almost killed himself catching a ball), and Roy Campanella, the star catcher. Many prominent people came in nightly to hear us play. It was great! I was really in heaven talking to and playing for these people.

Then conditions started to change, and restaurants were suffering because they were a luxury item. People didn't have the extra money to spend eating out. Mr. Sheen thought I should take a cut in salary because the restaurant wasn't doing too well and he couldn't afford the band. He didn't want us to leave, though, because his customers loved my group.

I agreed to a pay cut, but the third time he asked, I threatened to leave. He was skeptical about our ability get another job, so I bet him $200 that we would have another job within two weeks. I called General Artists Corporation (GAC) and spoke to Johnny Hamp, an agent I had worked for when he had a band in England. He called me back to say he had a hotel job in Atlantic City that I could start in five days. Not only did Sheen lose his bet, he lost his favorite orchestra. Milton Sheen was not a happy guy.

Good Gigs, Bad Bosses

After leaving Oetjen's in 1949, after three years, I landed some good gigs that would have been even better if the guys in charge had been more professional. One of them was in Atlantic City. Even though the hotel was a fine one, the Senator, which was at the ocean end of South Carolina Avenue, I wasn't too happy there because the boss was an obnoxious person who would take out his watch every time I started to work, making it obvious that he was timing how long I played.

Fed up with his uncivilized behavior, I called Johnny Hamp at GAC and told him how the boss behaved. He told me not to take it personally, just to ignore him, since he was like that with everyone who worked at the Senator.

That boss never changed. His watch came out every time I started to play. I couldn't wait to finish my engagement there. My contract was for twelve weeks, but it seemed like a hundred years had gone by before I finally finished the engagement. For my own reasons, though, I didn't storm out when I was through, though I may have felt like doing that. Instead, I went to the obnoxious boss and actually thanked him for giving me the opportunity to work there.

I always think it best to leave on a good note, no matter how badly behaved a boss has been. Burning bridges is a bad idea in this business, because you never know who you will encounter down the road.

My agent wasted no time in getting me another job right away, this one at Tony Yonadi's Homestead Golf and Country Club in Spring Lake Heights, New Jersey. Again, I was near the ocean, and again I worked under an obnoxious boss, a Mr. Bartholomew. Was it something in the water at the ocean in New Jersey that turned the bosses mean?

When that gig ended, I headed right for the union. I needed another job, but we had to break this pattern.

And boy, did we.

At Home with the Hoboken Crowd

The next job was much more my style. I was working with Bill Henry, a talented orchestra leader and trombonist, performing at the Shore Road Casino in Brooklyn, a big place with 1500 seats. Now this was the *right* kind of Jersey connection. It seems Bill was from Hoboken, Sinatra territory, hometown of Frank and his friends. Not only did Bill belong to that Hoboken crowd, but all of Bill's musicians did, too.

Though I was the odd man out, I fit right in. We were like family, because I had such a good history with Frank during our time with the Brooklyn Boys and later the great Harry James experience. We all hit it off great.

At the Casino, we had Johnny Buccini playing trumpet and Bill Henry playing trombone. Bill played trombone at the Tommy Dorsey level. In fact, Tommy gave Bill his own personal trombone as a

Christmas present one year. Then we had Benny Caruso on drums. Benny had been in the Army with me, and he had recommended me for this job. We also had a great sax section.

We were putting on a show.

Raised in Germany, Bill loved the way I played piano: I could segue from classical to jazz effortlessly, which is uncommon here in the states. He was even happier when he realized I could play anything he wanted to hear.

Eventually, I wrote arrangements and orchestrated for the band. That was a lot of fun.

I was now writing music with the new musical sounds I had learned. Some of these sounds I got a chance to try with some of the new performers just blossoming, such as Eddie Fisher, Julius La Rosa, Vaughn Monroe, and Don Cornell. I was really having a ball. Since they were all friends and trusted me, they were especially willing to try some of the new music I wrote.

I even had a chance to write for Eddie Manson, the harmonica genius who later became known for his high profile TV, radio, and movie soundtracks. Eddie had toured with the USO during the war. He'd get a good deal of exposure in later years on *The Ed Sullivan Show*, with Mitch Miller's orchestra, and other venues. If you heard a harmonica that sounded like dozens of other instruments at once, that was Eddie.

Eddie was one of the talented Juilliard classmates I mentioned earlier. At this point, he was just starting to create music for TV commercials with our other Juilliard classmate, the sparkling, always energetic Nanette Fabray. Nanette's career began even earlier than mine did. She was four years old as "Baby Nanette," a singing and tap dancing vaudevillian working with that era's top stars. She benefited from winning a scholarship to the school of her craft, just as I did, setting her up for a Tony-winning career in musical comedy.

I enjoyed catching Nanette on TV's *Hollywood Squares*, and was very proud of her earlier work as well, when she did the impossible in replacing the irreplaceable Imogene Coca, teaming up with Sid

Caesar in 1954. Nanette did not hide the fact that she was hearing-impaired while she was, but after four operations, she was able to hear. I think that challenging experience turned Nanette into a selfless champion of the handicapped. Eventually, she won the Eleanor Roosevelt Humanitarian Award.

The Big Conductor with the Little Mustache

Another of the great musical talents I was happy to find myself working with during these exciting years was Paul Whiteman, the first conductor with the good taste and foresight to conduct George Gershwin's magnificent, jazz-influenced *Rhapsody in Blue*, back in 1924. Whiteman had established a top-notch reputation as a dance bandleader during the twenties. He had twenty-eight ensembles all over the East Coast, sometimes consisting of thirty-five musicians, when other bands had only ten. He recorded many hit records during that decade, too, and was said to have earned a million dollars a year—in the twenties!

Whiteman was widely known as The King of Jazz, though some did dispute that title. Duke Ellington had no trouble agreeing with it, though, as he wrote in his autobiography: "Paul Whiteman was known as the King of Jazz, and no one as yet has come near carrying that title with more certainty and dignity."

Whiteman was also known for being able to blend symphonic music with jazz, a practice I identified with. This bandleader of ours was an imposing guy who cut an unusual figure, though sometimes his peculiar appearance struck me as funny. One particular night I was playing a Latin piece while Whiteman was accompanying me on the maracas. I happened to look over at him and he really looked strange—a huge person with such a small mustache, he could have been a walrus shaking those rattles. He resembled one of the sketches of him that used to appear so regularly in the newspapers that you could have thought he was a political figure. Paul Whiteman was a cartoonist's dream.

We in the Paul Whiteman Band were having a good time playing his highly orchestrated music, and there was every indication that our listeners were having a fine time too.

I was really riding high at this time! I was being paid a good salary as a staff member of the Whiteman orchestra because it was a union job.

Filling the Airwaves with Musical Fun

The Piano Playhouse was a Sunday morning radio show that I appeared on regularly, along with the great Cy Walter, who was variously known as "The Art Tatum of Park Avenue," "The Darling of New York Supper Clubs," and even "The Michelangelo of Music." Cy was both a jazz improvisationalist and a master of show tunes with a unique creative style. Stan Freeman would join us, as well. Stan was an Emmy award-winning pianist, composer, lyricist, arranger, conductor, and studio musician from Tex Beneki's big band, who later became a nightclub comic. His studio work was often heard backing Frank, Peggy, Ella, and the rest of the best. It's Stan's harpsichord you can hear backing up Rosemary Clooney on her hit "Come on-a My House." How could a show like that not be fun?

We played piano individually for the first part of the program, and then together for the final segment. The show featured such well-known artists as Percy Faith, Skitch Henderson, The Modernaires, and Helen Kress and her famous guitar-playing husband, Carl. So many performers joined us that, at times, The Piano Playhouse seemed like a Broadway showcase.

It was a great opportunity for me, meeting and playing for—and sometimes with—many of the greatest American musical stars.

I was getting more and more connected with people who were the best in the business, always grateful for the amazing opportunities I was given and for the training and dedication that enabled me to make the best of every opening.

Musicians are always looking forward to the opportunity that's yet to come, but what I didn't know was that my next job, a simple restaurant gig on Long Island, would bring me the most precious connection of all.

Chapter Eight
As the Forties End, My New Life Begins

WE SAW KEY CHANGES in the American music business in 1949. Seven-inch 45-rpm vinyl disks hit the market, replacing the old, breakable 78-rpm records that had been around since 1910. This was the beginning of a trend that's been taken to new limits today as our music machines keep getting smaller and smaller!

The other musical shift that occurred around the middle of the 20th century was the change in Big Band swing music that had dominated American culture for a decade beginning in the mid-1930s. The distinctive sound we made with Harry James, with its emphasis on the offbeat that had America dancing and screaming for more, the music that many say carried us through the war, was on its way out, sadly. It was definitely a pleasure for us musicians to produce the all-American Big Band sound and it was a joy for America to listen.

Several factors contributed to the decline of swing music. During the war we musicians were told that it was getting more and more difficult to staff a Big Band while guys were being drafted right and left. Given wartime economics, the cost of touring with a large ensemble became problematic. Smaller three-to-five-piece bands were more cost-effective and manageable.

There was another reason for the death of swing. Strikes by the musicians' unions prohibited a great deal of recording between 1942 and 1948. For example, no recordings were legally made in 1948, although major labels were bootlegging a little bit.

When the recording ban was finally lifted in January 1949, swing had evolved into new styles, such as bebop. Crooners like Sinatra, who grew their chops with the Big Bands, were singing pop music.

A Life-Changing Gig in Manhasset

I was happy to join the guys making recordings. One day in 1949 while talking to an old friend, I mentioned that I had just finished making a record with my group, The Dolph Traymon Trio. He asked if I had the recording with me. When I said yes, he asked if he could play it for his uncle, who owned a fine new restaurant in Manhasset, Long Island and was looking for a musical group to perform there. This was a lovely area, near where celebrities such as Perry Como lived.

My friend's uncle liked what he heard, and soon I was playing at Caro's, a particularly beautiful restaurant. I eventually would co-own Caro's, staying there for three more years, until I realized that you can never do your best unless the people around you are doing the same.

Little did I anticipate that I'd come away from Caro's restaurant with a lot more than applause and a good paycheck.

The group I brought with me to Caro's was the single finest trio I had ever worked with. It included Russ Hale, a drummer who had been in high school in Brooklyn with me, and Teddy Stevens, a bassist. Teddy (whose real name was Peter Ingoglia) was the father of my godchild, Connie Stevens (born Concetta Rosalie Ann Ingoglia). Connie became famous acting and singing. In a duet with Edd Byrnes, Connie scored a hit single with "Kookie, Kookie, Lend Me Your Comb," which first played on the popular TV series, *77 Sunset Strip*. Connie had many youth-oriented hits. She also proved to be one of our best babysitters.

Our trio spent quite a few years working at Caro's together, and we were like one big happy family.

Finding More than I Bargained for at Caro's

The patrons who came to Caro's liked our style of music; we soon gained a reputation for ourselves and gathered a substantial following. The atmosphere at Caro's was similar to the feeling you get when you're at the Fife 'n Drum today. There was a mirror over my keyboard so I could see who was coming into the restaurant while I played, in case I wanted to welcome them with "their" song. People definitely felt at home at Caro's.

One night just as we were about to begin, two young girls, Audrey Wrench and Eleanor Schmidt, appeared at the entrance, saying they wanted to come in to enjoy our music.

When Eleanor was permitted to drive her father's old car, she and her best friend, Audrey, headed out for adventure. They later told me that one night they found themselves at a burlesque show at Lake Ronkonkoma, walking in backward so nobody would see their faces. This night, when they landed at Caro's, the headwaiter came over to ask me if it would be all right to make an exception and let them in. I left the piano and went over to tell them that it was against policy to allow unescorted girls. Pleading they wanted only to hear us play, they promised to order sandwiches and leave as soon as they had finished eating. I went to the boss and asked if it was OK to let them in. Since it was not one of our busy nights, he agreed and the girls were seated.

One Sunday, about a month later, the girls came again, and again we made an exception so they could enjoy the music. I realized I was beginning to like this Audrey girl; there was truly something special about her. I boldly asked her if she was free the following night, Monday, our night off from Caro's. She said yes but that we couldn't get together until after she'd finished modeling.

I wasn't at all surprised that this beautiful girl was a model. It turns out she was the real thing, a graduate of the Barbizon School of Modeling. The school sent her to the best jobs. During the day she was busy walking the runway at fashion shows for wholesalers, representing Hattie Carnegie, Pauline Trigere, and other labels at the Waldorf and other fine venues, while another lucky pianist, the famed Ted Straeter, played his trademark song, "The Most Beautiful Girl in the World."

And she was.

A Marrying Kind of Girl

Fine, I said, "After you're finished modeling we'll get together."

And we did. Rather than go to a bar for drinks, we went to an ice cream parlor for ice cream sodas. That was appropriate because Audrey was only nineteen. I had just turned thirty.

It turned out to be a beautiful first date. We had a great conversation and things started looking up.

As I was driving home that night, I thought *This is the kind of girl I would like to marry.* After several more dates, I made up my mind. Audrey was definitely the girl for me.

I called and told her I wanted to marry her and said she had only four days to decide. She said, "Are you crazy? I'm only nineteen."

I replied, "I know how old you are, and you still have four days to make up your mind." She suggested that we take some time. So I agreed.

A week seemed more than time enough. I called her again and asked for a decision. She asked if we could meet to discuss it. "Of course," was my reply. Once again, I picked her up and we went to a restaurant where we talked about our future together. One of the reasons I was sure we could be happy is that we wanted the same things from life.

Finally, Audrey said yes. But there was a slight problem. Audrey was underage in New York, where you had to be twenty one to be married by civil authorities.

I called my friend, Harry Pisapia, and told him of our plight. He suggested that County Judge Lowell, whom he knew well, could probably marry us. Judge Lowell did so, in the Mineola Courthouse on November 21, 1949. Harry arranged a dinner afterward at the

St. Regis Hotel to celebrate our wedding. After the ceremony, Judge Lowell told us that all the couples he ever married wound up having happy lives together. With a smile, he said to us, "Don't mess up my record."

We certainly haven't.

From the Sublime to Rudy Vallee

That night we had a great time dancing the night away. It ended differently than most weddings, though. When it was time for us to leave the St. Regis, I took Audrey home to her mother's house, kissed her goodnight and said, "I'll call you from Buffalo after I get there."

I had a gig the next day. That's probably one reason why Audrey's father, at that point not the happiest father of the bride in the world, said to his daughter, "Lots of luck. You know you're marrying a gypsy. You'll never stop going on the road!"

Instead of a honeymoon, we had what I call a funnymoon. I headed upstate to work for Rudy Vallee, who had an engagement at the casino in Buffalo. Rudy Vallee was one of the crooners who became popular because they soothed people's anxieties during the Great Depression. Crosby was another. Rudy and his Connecticut Yankees had been quite popular during the 1930s, and his expression, "Hi Ho everybody—this is Rudy Vallee!" was his trademark.

Crooners like Rudy were supposed to be romantic, and maybe Rudy was, but he was also unbelievably cheap. When I told him I had gotten married the day before, he said, "Wonderful. I have a present for you, then." He went to his cabinet, took out a photo of himself and autographed it. "For Dolph, a great guy." Later I found out he had been married five times, and this was only my first, so maybe the bloom was off the rose as far as he and marriage were concerned.

Cheap? You know how cold it is in Buffalo? Well one day he and I were on our way to a hotel and we parked the car, as usual, in the parking lot. I was bundled up, but I noticed that as soon as we parked,

Rudy took his coat off and threw it in the back of the car.

"Rudy!" I said. "It's really cold out. Aren't you going to need your coat?" "Nah," he said. "You don't think I'm going to tip the coat check girl, do you?"

A few weeks later our engagements were finished and I was happy to leave Rudy and Buffalo. It's never comfortable being around an ego like that. Besides, I had a bride to go home to.

Good things had happened for me at Caro's, so I decided that was the place for me to work.

But I always had more than one iron in the fire, and this was a busy time. One of my best opportunities was when the American Broadcasting Company (ABC) offered me a job as a staff musician. I was now conductor, pianist, and arranger for their performers. This kind of job was known among musicians as among the best we could be offered. Unfortunately, the job was not permanent, so I left.

A Hit over the Airwaves

I had gotten to know the influential radio host Barry Gray when I was conducting the Army band, so when I had a record to promote, I took it to Barry at New York City's WOR. He liked it, and told me he'd put it on his playlist so it would be sold over the counter in music shops.

Barry did play it on the air. It got quite a response from the audience and we were now selling lots of records, as a result. By coincidence, it had the same title as my friend Peggy Lee's recording of "Mañana." I had played for Peggy at Basin Street East, and we'd become good friends. The difference between the two recordings was that mine was a piano solo and hers was a vocal. Later, I reminded her of the recording and she said my record was better.

The only thing Audrey and I needed now was a place to live. We looked at several apartments. They were so awful, they reminded us of tenements.

Audrey and I had so much going for us, we were very blessed. All we needed was our own house, since there were no apartments available to our liking. I guess we just weren't the apartment type. We were delighted and relieved, then, when my boss at Caro's, Mickey Ross, offered us the use of his beach house, which was empty at that time.

Audrey, our friend Teddy Stevens, and I went to look at the house, which was on a nice stretch of beach in Island Park, which really is an island though it's considered part of the town of Hempstead, Long Island. We all liked the house, and agreed that the three of us would temporarily live there. One good feature was that it was right near a Long Island Railroad station, making it easier for me to commute to ABC. At night, Teddy and I could easily drive to Caro's in Manhasset from Island Park.

We had some good laughs during those days. On the way home from the train station each night, Teddy and I passed a farm stand with a woodpile always standing in front of it, for some reason. We had a fireplace at the Island Park house, so at one point Teddy decided to take home some logs for us to burn.

We did this for several nights without a problem. One night a big hound dog came running from nowhere, just as Teddy was picking out our usual load of logs. You never saw a guy drop a bunch of wood all over the place and run for his life to the car faster than Teddy did that night. We pulled away as soon as he was in the car, as fast as lookout guys at a bank robbery. Later we would laugh every time we thought about that night and that dog coming out of the shadows after the neighborhood wood thief.

Enter Elissa and a New House

In 1953 we became a true family when Audrey gave birth to our daughter, Elissa, in Mineola General Hospital. She was a beautiful, sweet baby and she made us very happy.

Elissa got bigger. After a couple of years Audrey said she thought it might be time for us to have our own house. One afternoon we drove to Locust Valley on the north shore of Long Island, New York to look around. On Wood Lane we saw a corner property, about one-and-a-half acres on a hill and overlooking the entire surrounding area. Audrey loved this picturesque spot. We looked for a reputable builder, and found one. In 1953, we started to build our first house.

In the interim, while our house was being built, Audrey's mother, Florence, suggested we live with her in her New Hyde Park house. She had been living all alone after she and Audrey's father had separated. We gave it a try for the few months while our house was being built.

Finally our house was completed, and it was beautiful.

Audrey's mother sold her house, and the four of us moved into our wonderful new home. In 1957, Elissa gained a sister. Tracey, born in Glen Cove Hospital, was every bit as beautiful and sweet as her sister. We couldn't have been happier.

With Audrey's mother and our delightful new baby, we were indeed living in a perfect house to raise a growing family! Elissa and Tracey both went to Buckley Country Day School. Later, Elissa went to St. Margaret's High School while Tracey attended Westover.

We had a private beach where we could go swimming in the summertime, as well as have cookouts on our beach at night. Our kids, who loved living there, competed in swimming meets and stayed busy with all kinds of games. Our neighbors, who were full of stories and jokes, brought cookies for the children to enjoy. Audrey remembers filling out crossword puzzles on Sunday mornings. If she got stuck, she had only to call "65 down" and somebody a few beach blankets away would call back with the answer.

What a neighborhood!

It was fantastic living in Locust Valley. The six years we spent in that house were among the best of our early years.

Chic Country Clubs, Big City Clubs

It wasn't long before my band and I started playing the many leading, often newsworthy country clubs in the area. Living in the area made it so much easier for this to happen. We played at the Creek Club, Muttontown, Nassau, Glen Head, The Engineers Club, and the famous Piping Rock, noted for being the unfortunate site of Cole Porter's life-changing riding accident in 1937.

I felt like I was the King of the Society Bands during these days. It was hard work, however! I'd open up with "From This Moment On" and close with "The Party's Over," but it would be a long time between those two songs, believe me. It was always the longest possible day because society bands are expected to provide continuous music, taking as few breaks as possible Also, I often had a gig in the afternoon as well as the one at night. That can be tiring. But make no mistake, I enjoyed that life. I had a social secretary who arranged my connections with the various clubs, which was a tremendous help.

One of the places I played during the week was the Stork Club, one of the most famous nightclubs in the world, called "New York's New Yorkiest Place" by the powerful newspaper columnist Walter Winchell. It's ironic that the club was the very symbol of café society, and yet Sherman Billingsley, the owner, was an ex-bootlegger from Enid, Oklahoma who partnered with two gamblers to open the club in 1929, of all years. The gamblers later sold their shares to a guy who was a front for mobsters who, at one point, actually kidnapped Billingsley for ransom. (Only in New York!) The club was at its third and final location when I played there, 3 East 53rd, just east of Fifth. This location is now Paley Park.

The Ace of Clubs

The Stork Club had a 14-carat gold chain across its front door, with admission possible only if the doorman approved.

When the Stork Club first opened, writer Heywood Broun, a member of the Algonquin Round Table, mistook the club for a funeral parlor. He came in, took off his hat, and piously walked to the back, only to find, instead of a body, a bar. The bar was to his liking, so he invited his influential friends and the Stork Club was born.

My audience at the Stork Club consisted of movie stars, celebrities, the wealthy, showgirls, and aristocrats, all together. Theater people came because of Billingsley's longtime paramour, Ethel Merman. Billingsley assigned a waiter exclusively to Merman, whose sole job was to light her cigarettes.

The list of Stork Club habitués included some known throughout the world by their first names—Tallulah, Bing, Judy, Marilyn, Grace, Frank, and so on. And then there were the heavy-duty last names, Kennedy, Hoover, Hemingway, Salinger, Vanderbilt, Chaplin, Windsor, Lamour. But the club was even more noteworthy for those Billingsley chose to exclude. They included Milton Berle, Elliott Roosevelt, Humphrey Bogart, and Jackie Gleason. The club's "Cub Room" was also known as "The Snub Room," guarded by a captain they called "St. Peter." Then there were the Main Dining Room, the bar, a private room for parties, and a couple of other rooms.

For public relations reasons, savvy Billingsley kept people on staff whose sole job was to listen to the guests' chatter, separate fact from rumor, and report facts to columnists.

Billingsley always treated me well, but he reserved his true largess for his guests, who were famously treated to amazing gifts, such as diamond-studded compacts, French perfumes, champagne, and even automobiles. Every regular club patron received a case of champagne at Christmas.

I also played piano at John Perona's equally noteworthy club El Morocco, which had begun as a speakeasy during the Depression and was the first nightclub to use a velvet rope at the door. My piano was directly in front of the orchestra. There was usually at least one female celebrity who tried to impress the musicians with how great she looked. Her dancing partner usually gave a $100 tip to the orchestra, not uncommon in good clubs in those days.

El Morocco was even more sophisticated than the Stork Club. It was known for its trademark zebra-striped banquettes, easily identifiable in the photos of celebrities that appeared almost daily in the newspapers. It was very clever, that zebra design, since it left no doubt where the celebrity had been photographed the night before. It was even more clever of the club to ensure that a photographer was on the scene every night.

At El Morocco, Vanderbilts and Astors could be seen seated near Cary Grant, Marlene Dietrich, and Jackie Kennedy, as well as the notorious playboy Porfirio Rubirosa, who famously dallied with Monroe, Hayworth, Gabor, and even Eva Peron.

Connecticut Governor Jodi Rell with me at the Fife 'n
Drum on Dolph Traymon Day, February 8, 2009.

My brother, Joseph Tramontana,
with his partner, Louise Santos.

My late sister, Adele P. Ortiz,
with her husband, Gabe, in
1979.

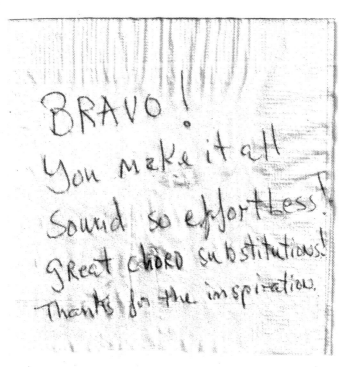

BRAVO!
You make it all
Sound so effortless!
Great chord substitutions!
Thanks for the inspiration.

Whether written spontaneously on cocktail napkins or in formal notes, my friends and customers have been so generous over the years, offering the warm support that means so much to me and keeps me playing.

We all loved your concert! It was a smash! And aren't we glad that nice man came down from Woodbury to tune the cranky piano! You made it sing! Happy New Year to you all — Midge & Tom

A slightly sunburned Audrey, the best gift
my piano playing ever gave me.

This impressive guest played the bagpipes as he entered the
restaurant to celebrate the thirtieth anniversary of the Fife 'n Drum.

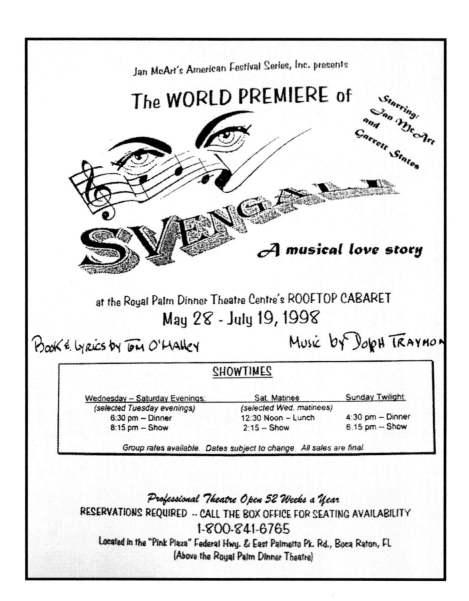

Jan McArt's American Festival Series, Inc. presents

The WORLD PREMIERE of

Starring Jan McArt and Garrett States

SVENGALI

A musical love story

at the Royal Palm Dinner Theatre Centre's ROOFTOP CABARET

May 28 - July 19, 1998

Book & Lyrics by Tom O'Malley   Music by Dolph Traymon

SHOWTIMES		
Wednesday – Saturday Evenings:	Sat. Matinee	Sunday Twilight:
(selected Tuesday evenings)	*(selected Wed. matinees)*	
6:30 pm – Dinner	12:30 Noon – Lunch	4:30 pm – Dinner
8:15 pm – Show	2:15 – Show	6:15 pm – Show

Group rates available. Dates subject to change. All sales are final.

Professional Theatre Open 52 Weeks a Year
RESERVATIONS REQUIRED -- CALL THE BOX OFFICE FOR SEATING AVAILABILITY
1-800-841-6765
Located in the "Pink Plaza" Federal Hwy. & East Palmetto Pk. Rd., Boca Raton, FL
(Above the Royal Palm Dinner Theatre)

Three distinct facets of my musical life. Svengali was my second fling with musical theater. It was fun working with French firecracker Denise Darcel as I conducted my orchestra in Hong Kong. And I borrow from every musical genre I know and love when I perform concerts for some very worthy local causes.

Chapter Nine
Multitasking Before It Was Trendy

AS AUDREY LIKES TO SAY, "Dolph's played for the crowned heads of Europe and the bald heads of New York."

I've always been able to juggle musical jobs. It's one of the things musicians learn to do and it keeps things interesting. For instance, I was on the air several evenings a week on radio station WOR in New York City, while at the same time I was working at an elegant French-Italian restaurant at 13 East 55th Street in Manhattan. L'Aiglon opened in 1919 and was known for the notables who frequented it.

I played the downstairs club at L'Aiglon. Judy Garland, always with her retinue, would parade through the room, then head for the upstairs room where she would sing. Carlos Ramirez, one of the most important Colombian singers of all time walked through my room, singing the song he used to open his act.

My listening audience at L'Aiglon was star-studded, as in true aristocrats, not the red carpet type. One frequent L'Aiglon visitor was Serge Obolensky, whose original name was Sergei Platonovich, 5th Knyaz Obolensky-Neledinsky-Meletzky, a Russian prince who first married a daughter of the Czar and later the daughter of John Jacob Astor. At fifty-three, he had been the US Army's oldest paratrooper and, at another point, vice chairman of the board of Hilton Hotels.

The list of Russian nobility I played for at L'Aiglon didn't end there. Most important to me as an appreciative audience was television personality Igor Cassini. He was the younger brother of Oleg, the fashion designer who dressed Jackie Kennedy. Igor was the second "Cholly Knickerbocker," influential society columnist for Hearst, including New York's *Journal-American,* writing a column he often generously and graciously filled with praise for my music. This delighted the restaurant's owner, Al Sirna, who knew he could expect an increase in customers whenever Cassini's raves about me appeared.

Cassini produced the *Celebrity Register,* and not only did he belong to the Jet Set, he coined that phrase to describe his generation's more global version of Café Society. His first wife, Bootsie, later married William Randolph Hearst, keeping everything in the family, I guess.

This fascinating Russian first experienced the glare of American national attention in a highly unusual way, in 1939, when he wrote a column in Virginia that upset high society there. Instead of taking the high road, the upper crust took decidedly low-class revenge. In a story that's hard to believe now, the Virginia aristocracy engaged a trio of locals to kidnap Cassini and, unbelievably, tar and feather this nobleman, making him national news overnight.

The Hearst Connection Lives On

When my contract was up at L'Aiglon, I went to work at the Warwick Hotel, yet another Hearst connection, being the grand yet intimate European-style oasis that William Randolph Hearst built for his love, Marion Davies. It was situated opposite the Ziegfeld Theater for a reason: Hearst wanted the Warwick to house his theater-going friends.

At the Warwick I enjoyed playing opposite the Page Cavanaugh Trio, which had a Nat King Cole style sound to it. Page was a jazz and pop pianist, a vocalist and arranger who had met his guitarist, Al Viola, and his bassist, Lloyd Pratt, in the military. "Walkin' My Baby Back Home" and "All of Me" were two of their hits. They were originally from Hollywood, where they played most of their engagements.

I enjoyed playing the Warwick and worked there for several months.

I was commuting to Manhattan by train every night but the Long Island Railroad's off-schedule trains made me late for work on several occasions. The hotel manager was a stickler for punctuality and berated me every time I was late. He refused to consider the distance I was traveling and that unforeseen events caused the delay.

One night I was ten minutes late, but for an unusual and undeniably dramatic reason: the train I was on hit an automobile. This certainly might have made any late excuse legitimate, but the manager refused to accept my reason, saying, "You are supposed to start promptly at seven p.m. Because you are late, I don't want you to go on tonight. Let the Page Cavanaugh Trio go on instead."

There was a fantastic violinist, Fred Fassler, who had a little show on Channel 5. Though he played in another part of the restaurant, he often listened to my work and really appreciated it. After overhearing the boss's response to me, Fred went to him and said, "You don't punish performers like Dolph. He is too good a musician and deserves more consideration than that. Many of your customers like him and look forward to hearing him play." The boss recanted and told me to go on as usual.

Disrespect leaves a bad taste no matter how elegant the surroundings. I was glad when my contract ended at the beautiful Warwick.

Hootenannies and Hobby Horses... Me?

Meyer Horowitz, who had seen me play at the Warwick Hotel, invited me to work for him at the Village Barn, which he had opened in 1930 at 52 W. 8th Street in Greenwich Village. It was well-known. Later, after it closed, it became the world renowned Electric Lady recording studio, made famous by such as Jimi Hendrix.

Much earlier, Rudy Vallee ran a nearby club called Villa Valee. He had discovered Judy Canova at the Village Barn. Canova sang, yodeled, and played guitar and was typed as a wide-eyed likable country bumpkin, often barefoot and wearing her hair in braids, sometimes topped with a straw hat, so the Barn was a perfect place for her. Don Cornell, an Italian from the Bronx with a robust, smooth baritone, got his start at the Village Barn though he was a little difficult to picture there.

With my radically different musical experience, the Village Barn, a country music nightclub, was totally out of character for me. But Meyer wanted me there and I went, even though I was still doing nightly broadcasts on WOR, CBS, and sometimes NBC at that time.

I can give you an idea of the place by describing its wine list. The illustration had one woman milking a cow and another with a martini glass. The caption was "Pink Lemonade from Contented Cows." The Village Barn was an unusual place. They played all sorts of games, including turtle races and hobby horse. (And yes, I did play piano to accompany a hobby horse race.) A master of ceremonies ran all the games. It was a lot of fun and the people who left each evening always said they had a great evening out.

There was liquor served at the Village Barn, but no bar, since Meyer didn't like bars. The Barn also didn't have a piano at first, but Meyer wanted me there so he brought one in. It was a fantastic piano he had inherited from his mother and was dying to hear me play. That piano had a wonderful sound and I enjoyed playing it.

Caro's Proves You Can Go Home Again

It was time to get back to one of my favorite all-time places, Caro's in Manhasset, where I met Audrey. No wonder I was always drawn back there: it was a fabulous place to work, with an unbelievable list of illustrious clientele that included such stars as Perry Como. I accompanied Perry on several numbers, usually after he was given some encouragement from his friends and golfing buddies. Another entertainer who frequented the place was Jackie Richards, a Broadway comic well-known for his comedy routine mimicking Danny Thomas and many famous orchestra leaders and musicians.

Other famous artists who frequented Caro's regularly were the great Tony Martin, Larry Clinton, and Carmen Cavallaro. Larry, also from Brooklyn, was a trumpeter and prominent bandleader who also played trombone and clarinet and was a great success as an arranger for the Dorseys, Louis Armstrong, and Bunny Berigan. Larry became popular by swinging the classics, but quit the music business at the start of WWII to become a pilot at the rank of captain. After being stationed in Calcutta and in China, he came back after the war to being a bandleader.

Carmen Cavallero was known as "The Poet of the Piano" for his rippling arpeggios and for translating such classics as Chopin's *Polonaise* into a pop idiom. There seemed to be a lot of that crossover music going on. Carmen, too, had played with Rudy Vallee and had also formed his own five-piece band early on, becoming a high-profile society bandleader. He produced a number of records for Decca and was popular at the Waldorf.

He was a nice fellow who played a mean piano, but he lacked polish. His orchestra had lots of class, but he had none.

Carmen, who was said to be influenced by Eddie Duchin, had the honor of recording the piano music for actor Tyrone Power. Carmen played the music portrayed by Power's hands while Power portrayed the man himself in *The Eddie Duchin Story*. Eddie's son, Peter, later said the story depicted in the film was largely fiction.

Eddie Duchin, the Standard-Bearer

Eddie was one of my all time favorite musicians and a good friend. He used to frequent Caro's in the early days when he wasn't playing with Leo Reisman's orchestra at the Central Park Casino, an upscale night-club. Eddie died of leukemia in 1951, much too early at only forty-one years, after being one of the earliest pianists to lead a commercially successful large band. He became one of the most popular pianists and bandleaders of the thirties and forties, famous for his engaging onstage personality and his classy piano style. He'd play his piano cross-handed, using only one finger on the lower hand.

A former Navy man, Eddie had served as a combat officer in a destroyer squadron in the Pacific, and left as a lieutenant commander. Now this was a guy who was every bit as elegant as his piano playing. Can you believe he never had any formal musical training?

Eddie was usually at Caro's on Sunday nights when he would bring along his young son, Peter, and the nanny. Peter later followed in his dad's footsteps. Eddie was returning to the music business from his service in the Navy, and had formed an orchestra, which was about to open at the Waldorf Astoria. He said, "Why don't you and Audrey come to see me on my opening night? I'll set up a reservation for you."

I was excited to go; it seemed like a great evening out for Audrey and me, and I would get to just listen to music for a change.

The gorgeous room where Eddie was playing was just as elegant as I imagined it would be. I gave the maitre'd my name and told him that our reservation had been made by Mr. Duchin. The maitre d' seemed none too pleased, for some reason.

After supposedly looking in the reservations book, he returned and said, "I don't see any reservation in the book for you." Disappointed and baffled, we were planning to leave, thinking we would come another night.

Just then I saw Eddy finishing a set and coming off the bandstand. I approached him. "Did you get your table?" he asked.

When I told him somebody apparently forgot to enter it into the reservations book, he was furious. He went to the maitre'd and said, "Listen, when I make a reservation for someone, I expect it to be honored. Please set up a table near the dance floor with three chairs so I can join my friend and his wife. If this occurs again, I'll have you working in the basement."

Without further ado a special table was brought in and set up for the three of us. It turned out to be a wonderful evening, and we were able to have a nice, uninterrupted conversation with Eddie.

When he returned to the bandstand, Audrey and I danced to his wonderful music.

When musicians happen to be among the guests at a musically oriented place, it is customary to invite them to sit in to play a few numbers. It was no different at Caro's. The music never stopped. It was usual for me to leave at four in the morning after one of these sessions. No surprise that Caro's earned a reputation as a lively, fun place to go.

Notable non-musicians came to Caro's, such as Alfred and Bill Leavitt, who built Levittown, and Sol Atlas, who built the New York Stock Exchange and gave great parties at his huge mansion in Kings Point, Long Island.

One brilliant non-musician regular at Caro's was Peter Arno, the renowned cartoonist whose instantly recognizable work appeared in the *New Yorker* from the mid-twenties until the late sixties, depicting a cross-section of New York high society.

One night at Caro's a woman was giving me a particularly hard time. When I mentioned it to Peter, he said, "I'll take care of her" and, with that, he drew a sketch of a man and woman having sex and handed it to her. The woman was so embarrassed, she left, and never returned. On another occasion, Peter noticed a male customer acting obnoxiously, so high-class Peter Arno (Hotchkiss, Yale) walked up to the guy and, calmly unzipping his fly, urinated in his lap. The man, thinking he was so drunk that he had wet himself, paid his check and left in a hurry.

Chapter Ten
My Dueling Steinways and a One-Night Stand with Broadway

EARLY EACH MORNING I rode the train into New York to do my radio and television shows at ABC. At the same time, I was also A&R man for Jubilee Records, which was founded by Jerry Blaine. A&R means "artists and repertoire." I headed the division of the label responsible for talent scouting and overseeing the artistic development of the label's recording artists. I also acted as liaison between artists and the label, responsible for every activity involving artists up to and after the album's release.

The guys in our neighborhood were successful business people and some of their wives were industry executives too. Audrey was in sales and still working as a model. She sometimes joined us on the morning train.

One neighbor, Bill Mellor, worked at ABC as a newscaster in the News Division, and took the same morning train as I did. Sometimes Mellor's wife, Honor, would join us on her way to work as a leading fashion model. We had a fine group to talk to in the morning.

One morning a friend happened to mention that the Byrd Estate in Oyster Bay was having an auction, and among the items listed was a Steinway grand piano. People from all over the world were expected to participate. Would I be interested? I indicated I would but unfortunately the time for the auction was inconvenient. Harold Weicker, Governor Weicker's brother, offered to stand in for me.

Initially the auction started in the estate's garage, where they were auctioning fifteen vintage cars of all makes, including Packards, several Mercedes, and even an old Stutz Bearcat. When they got to the pianos, there was a great deal of interest. Harold called to report to me, and said, "Dolph, I have good news and bad news. Yes, you did get the Steinway. In fact you got two Steinways, because they were auctioned as a package."

Well, I may have wanted the Steinway, but not two of them.

We had been living in our Woods Lane house in Locust Valley for several years, in somewhat cramped conditions. We felt the need to seek larger quarters because we had two children and my mother-in-law was living with us. We already had one Steinway, and now with the other two, we had three.

We placed two in the living room, back to back and the other one in our den. It was clearly time to approach one of my friends, a Realtor, with regard to buying a larger house. He knew of one that was for sale; the owner's wife was seriously ill, and he wasn't sure whether the owner had put the house on the market but he promised to see if it was available.

He called several days later and said he had made arrangements with the owner to have us look at the house, located on a hill in Locust Valley, opposite the famous Piping Rock Country Club.

Home for My Steinway Triplets

Audrey and I went to see the place and loved it. It was quite a house, a two-story colonial on three-and-a-half acres. We left with the understanding that the owner would call us if he wanted to sell.

After several weeks passed, we received a call that the house was available. Audrey, my two daughters, and I went to see the house once more. The owner was taken by the charm of our two girls, and we worked out a deal to purchase his place, making plans to sell our old house.

It was 1964. Unfortunately, it was a bad time to try to sell our house. I asked if the owner could give me three months more time. I also asked if he would give me a second mortgage for one year. He asked us to let him think about it and give him time to talk to his attorney.

The owner had a son who did not want the house. A week later the call came.

"You can have the house and you can have one year to close on it."

Audrey and I were thrilled and arranged to move into our new home.

We signed all the papers and closed the deal. Unfortunately, a few months after his wife passed away, the owner also died. The money we paid went to his estate.

After we moved in and placed our furniture in the various rooms, we placed the two new Steinway pianos back to back at one end of our large living room, which was twenty-three feet long and thirty-five feet wide. The pianos looked fantastic there. We sold our original Steinway to Sammy Kaye's pianist.

It was 1964. After being so fortunate with all our homes, here we were living in another house that we dearly loved. Like the others, it appeared just when we needed it, though it did take three years until we finally sold our old house on Woods Lane.

Setting My Sights on Broadway

BMI (Broadcast Music, Inc.), the outfit that handles royalties for songwriters, has been offering a highly respected Musical Theater Workshop since 1961, dedicated to creating new writers and composers for this great American art form. I heard about the workshop at ABC. I auditioned, and was accepted into the workshop, which at that tune was still being taught by the dean of American musical conductors, Lehman Engel.

Though relatively new then, the course has since nurtured such shows as *A Chorus Line, Little Shop of Horrors, Nine, Once on This Island,* and even *The Book of Mormon.* Students of the Workshop explore the basics of writing for the musical theater through a series of assignments culminating in the creation of a ten-minute musical presented at year's end.

The second year of the Workshop results in the creation of a full-length musical. Participants are invited based on highly competitive auditions; mine involved earlier work I had done for the theater. These days, CDs are used to demonstrate what artists can do. As you can imagine, theater hopefuls apply to the Musical Theater Workshop from all over the country.

It is, and always was free of charge, so it was impossible to buy your way into it. It was a tough course, and the students really had to toe the line. After we prepared our work, we had to present it before the students, who acted as our critics. They were not particularly kind in their criticism, and that was good, since it forced us to do our best. Classes lasted for a year, and I studied several years with Lehman.

A Musical with a Tragic Ending

I teamed up at the Workshop with the talented writer Tom O'Malley, who was putting together book and lyrics for a musical he called *South of Heaven.* It was an all-black (everyone used the term "Negro" then) show that took place in the South. Tom had asked Juanita Hall, another Juilliard graduate who had famously starred in *Flower Drum Song* and played Bloody Mary in *South Pacific,* if she would be interested in starring. Juanita was excited, especially since it called for an all-black cast.

As a blues singer, Juanita was used to being backed by the likes of Coltrane and Doc Cheatham, and I was delighted to have the opportunity to work with this dynamic, highly experienced singer.

Juanita brought star-quality talent with her to our cast, including Billie Dee Williams, who was impressive in *A Taste of Honey* and the film, *The Last Angry Man.* Juanita also brought Dorothy Dandridge, who lost the Golden Globe for *Porgy and Bess* to Marilyn Monroe. Dorothy was a seasoned nightclub singer who had recorded with

Jimmy Lunceford and Oscar Peterson. She certainly added musical firepower to our stage.

Juanita also invited Roscoe Lee Browne, whose fine, rich baritone and dignified bearing you'd recognize immediately as his. What an amazing, multitalented guy! Champion runner, college professor, Shakespearean actor, who gained a reputation as the voice of an evil robot in *Logan's Run*, Roscoe was also a director who later won an Emmy and an Obie.

How could we lose?

Now with the casting at that elevated level, all we needed was a producer and the money to go ahead. We did several auditions for some backers. This process is far from new. Musicals bound for Broadway are especially costly, and they always were, even back in the sixties. To begin rehearsals and build sets, you must spark interest from potential investors, also called "angels." To do so, you need to stage one or more auditions for potential backers, private, staged readings of all or part of your show, with minimal accompaniment, props and costumes. When Richard Rodgers and Oscar Hammerstein teamed up to create *Oklahoma* in 1943, the composers had to endure dozens of backers' auditions before they had enough money to go into production, despite the cast's sterling reputations.

Though our backers' audition was well received, we heard no reassuring go-aheads.

The Backers Get It Back

During a television appearance, I met one of the nicest guys in television, Durward Kirby, announcer and host of the popular *Garry Moore Show*. At 6' 4" he was a familiar face to most of us at that time. When I told him about *South of Heaven*, Durward loved the idea and arranged a backers' audition for us at the Westchester Broadway Theater in Elmsford, New York. About a thousand people attended.

This dramatic story should have had a happy ending. Unfortunately, it didn't. One of the principals got greedy and the backers' money ended up in the wrong pockets, which is a huge no-no in the theater business. To make it worse, a personal relationship mixed with a business relationship made it difficult to clear things up.

Everybody wound up losing—the excellent cast, the theater-going public, the enthusiastic backers, and myself. We ended up having to do a very difficult thing: return the backers' money to the backers.

I did not hear from Tom O'Malley for several years, until he wrote me a note asking if I would be interested in a new musical he had written called *Svengali.*

We started all over again, trying out the show at St. Andrew's Church Auditorium in Kent. It was well received but economic conditions had changed and it was no longer so easy to obtain financing for a major theatrical production.

These are the experiences that turn a guy into a realist. All of a sudden, the idea of walking out of the orchestra pit, leaving the bright lights and the applause where they belong and going back to my first love, the piano, was looking really good to me.

Chapter Eleven
"The Band Went Haywire and the Audience Went Wild"

ONE DAY MY AGENT SAID, "Let's get you on *Arthur Godfrey's Talent Scouts*. It's a contest I think you can win." Godfrey was one of the most important radio hosts on record and a major player during the first decade of American TV, earning a million dollars a year, which was extraordinary for the time. He didn't just host one program; he ran a daily radio show and two top-ten prime-time TV shows, all for CBS. Early in his career Godfrey had noticed that most radio guys felt it necessary to put on a fake, deep, serious voice when that red light went on, and he bet that people were ready for a deep, microphone-friendly voice that spoke, instead, in a conversational tone, with some folksiness on the side. He was right.

Godfrey even went so far as to make fun of his sponsors, such American classics as Lipton Tea. TV-watching America was captivated by this freckle-faced, ukelele-playing, easygoing guy with the wide grin and unruly red hair. Godfrey had boosted the careers of Pat Boone, Tony Bennett, Eddie Fisher, my dear friend and godchild Connie Stevens, Patsy Cline…and Julius LaRosa, but that's a whole other story. The quality of talent Godfrey entertained was top-notch. I was delighted to be among them.

Arthur Godfrey's Talent Scouts was a fixture on Monday nights at 8:30 p.m. I went on the show and played the piano. My agent was right. I did win first prize. As he usually did with winners, Godfrey booked me for a week on his TV show, *Arthur Godfrey and His Friends*.

I played special arrangements I had written, accompanied by the show's large orchestra. After performing my solos, Godfrey praised my playing and predicted a great future for me. I felt honored.

Following my success on the Godfrey shows, I was booked on *Kay Kyser's College of Musical Knowledge,* a popular radio program on the NBC network. A bandleader and entertaining radio host, Kay chose to use the sound of his middle initial as a first name. His show combining a quiz with music, was on NBC radio for ten years. One of his catchphrases was "C'mon, chillen. Let's dance!"

I enjoyed working with a large orchestra behind me for that appearance. After I finished playing, Mr. Kyser gave me a gift of a suede jacket from a famous Hollywood store, along with a full set of Michelin tires for the Jaguar XKE I had just purchased. That Jag was my pride and joy. I rode around in it like a Hollywood bigshot.

On a radio roll, I was soon approached by a representative of radio station KMOX in Manhasset, Long Island with regard to doing a weekly broadcast from Caro's. The program was to have Dean Pepin as the announcer and Ham O'Hara, a noted sound effects genius, as the engineer. Pepin later became a well-known minister, a pastor who now hosts *The Miracle Hour* on the Internet. The KMOX show was a half-hour long and featured my playing along with several guest performers.

I loved doing that show, which was on the air for almost a year. It gave me a terrific chance to demonstrate my talent.

Why You Should Listen to Your Mother

One day the owner of Caro's came to me and said that his partner wanted to quit the restaurant business because his wife was unhappy. Would I be interested in purchasing his share? I went to visit my mother and told her. As usual, she wasn't shy about offering her opinion. "Are you crazy? You don't know these people. I don't think you should do it."

I didn't listen to my mother and went right ahead, buying a one-third interest in the restaurant for $30,000. I was now part owner of the best restaurant on Long Island.

My mother turned out to be right, of course. I started getting wind of the fact that things were not on the up-and-up, things were going on that didn't fit my way of doing business, but I couldn't prove anything. Another partner sold his share and got out. I was sort of stuck. I stayed with the business for quite some time, and eventually asked one of the principals to buy me out, which he said he would. But people's characters don't change, and I was never able to collect. He said he didn't have the money, and that was that.

That was the end of our time at Caro's.

What a lesson.

It was also the end of our trio, which broke up when Teddy Stevens went west to join his daughter, Connie Stevens, who was performing on *The Bob Hope Show*. Teddy asked me to come with them to California, but moving my family wasn't in the cards.

I said no.

Accompanying "The Queen"

An old friend, Russ Gary, came to see me one day while I was playing at New York's Americana Hotel to propose a tour of the Far East for me. He had become an agent for Theatrical Productions in the Far East, and wanted me to go to Japan as conductor as well as pianist for several shows. I would have to perform one show nightly and conduct the orchestra for the shows' stars. The only hitch was getting a work passport to enter Japan. It was so difficult—it took me almost a year before I was successful.

In the meantime, I was still playing the top nightclubs in New York, performing on TV, and accompanying various celebrities.

One of my very favorites was the legendary Peggy Lee, who became a good friend of mine. Peggy might have been Miss Sophistication when she sang—after all, no less than Duke Ellington named her "The Queen." But to her fellow musicians she was down-to-earth and unassuming. Born Norma Deloris Egstrom before a radio station manager changed her name, Peggy was a Scandinavian who grew up near Fargo, having to work on neighbors' farms to help support her family. Her father was a railroad station agent and her mother died when Peggy was very young. After a run-in with a car and a team of horses when she first learned to drive, she never drove a car again.

I played for Peggy at La Vie en Rose and Basin Street East, where her appearances became showbiz legend. She always sold out the club. Even in one of New York's worst blizzards, people lined up around the block to hear her. In a profile for NPR radio, her daughter Nicki remembered, "The city was shut down. We didn't think anyone would be there, but they came on foot, on sleds, by horse-drawn carriage!"

Such was the drawing power of Peggy Lee.

The very influential critic Leonard Feather wrote this in *Downbeat* during our heyday at La Vie en Rose:

Being very cautious about overstatement, we will only say conservatively that Peggy gave the greatest performance we have seen delivered by a singer in a Manhattan club in the last five years—and that includes everybody, male or female, from Lena Horne and Sinatra on down… Peggy does for a song what Jane Russell does for a sweater. If you only know Peggy Lee from records, or radio and TV and theaters, catch her sometime in an intimate nightclub. If you don't get a thrill—Jack, you must be dead.

"A Jammed Room and an Electric Singer"

Peggy gave our sold-out audiences such great songs as "I've Got You Under My Skin," "Lover," "Why Don't You Do Right," "My Heart Belongs to Daddy," "Good Morning Heartache," "Hard-Hearted Hannah," and "Mañana," with lyrics by Peggy herself.

Bill Smith, writing in *Billboard*, really captured the way it was in one of the great clubs during the fifties, with that great singer at the microphone:

"The jammed room saw Peggy Lee, an electric singer with a driving beat on some songs and a sensual appeal on torcheroos... Whatever it was, she has never sung so well nor sold as strongly as she did here. 'Lover'... built and built; the band went haywire, the gal gave it a mad jam session interpretation, and the audience went wild. It was one of those shows that happen rarely. Only a top-flight act could follow her that night."

In a book about the Big Bands, Peggy was quoted: "Band singing taught us the importance of interplay with musicians. We had to work close to the arrangement. Even if the interpretation of a particular song wasn't exactly what we wanted, we had to make the best of it. ...I will say this: I learned more about music from the men I worked with in bands than I've learned anywhere else. They taught me discipline and the value of rehearsing and how to train."

Peggy was married—she would ultimately get to husband number four—but if you want my opinion, her best choice was Dave Barbour, her first, who wrote songs with her and had been Benny Goodman's guitarist when she sang with Benny. The rest of the husbands seemed like all the wrong guys, losers who did nothing for Peggy but spend her money. One became her manager and one her press agent. They left her such a mess that eventually that nice lady was brought to financial ruin.

Before Peggy went onstage every night, she liked me to give her a hug and a kiss on the cheek, and to reassure her that she'd do a great job by saying, "Believe me, they will love you."

And, of course they always did. Miss Peggy Lee was a great star, a sweetheart of a gal, and a treasured friend.

I left La Vie en Rose and Basin Street East when my Japanese passport came through. As exciting as club work was, it was also tiring and rarely the only job I was doing, whether on the air or off. I was now forty-seven years old, not nineteen.

It was 1967 and soon I was on my way to Tokyo where the gigs would be easier. Leaving my family was never easy, especially to go to the other side of the world.

I played in all the major cities in the Far East, starting with the Copacabana nightclub in Tokyo. I was traveling with Dennis Como, Perry Como's nephew, who sang and played guitar. I thought he would be a great attraction, but he was a problem child. His ego was killing him. He gave everyone grief, including his new bride, a nice girl who would come to me crying and ultimately divorce him. She deserved better. He would even give me a problem at rehearsals, when he'd be performing onstage before I even entered the room. What kind of a way is that to rehearse? Dennis's father was no help. He was Perry Como's road manager, and thought he knew it all.

The Far East tour was a series of small stops. We played Okinawa one day and then traveled to Taipei the next and then on to the impressive President Hotel in Bangkok for a few days, then to Hong Kong.

I thought this was going to be easy. However, the best was yet to come later when we would be joined by a well-known actress.

What a list of exotic names we were scheduled to visit during the following few weeks: Nagoya, Osaka, Kowloon, Yokohama.

One day in Okinawa stands out, and it has nothing to do with my work. Taking a much-needed day off, I went swimming on a beach one sunny afternoon. It was fantastic. I was the only one on the beach, and it felt like Neverland. As I swam, my only concern was for the sharks in the water. The birds flying overhead were huge. What a magical afternoon! I have never been able to duplicate it.

The tour was actually exhausting, since it consisted of brief stops.

One thing is undeniable. We were beautifully received wherever we performed in the Far East.

We saw wonderful sights. In Thailand, the houses built along the Klong, the Thai name for canal, were all three-sided, with one side completely open. Their customs are as different from ours as their houses. One morning I saw a young girl come out of one of the houses, take off her sari, and slip into the dirty water to take a bath. I got accustomed to taking off my shoes and putting on visitor's slippers while visiting temples. I also stopped by the home of Jim Thompson, the famous fabric designer who founded the silk industry there. He had lived in Bangkok for many years before his death. He and his work were featured at the 1939 World's Fair.

I had a date to play at the Yusam Club in Korea. At the airport, I saw a woman trying to lift a satchel onto the counter. It looked heavy, so I gave her a hand. It turns out she was a major buyer for gems in the Far East, and invited me to join her for champagne after my concert. We sat and talked. The next day she asked how I would like to accompany her on a buying trip. I knew this would be interesting, so we went to a house in town, and there on the dining room table they had laid out hundreds of diamonds and all kinds of gems. I picked a few that I thought I could use with my tuxedo shirt, making a deal for four studs as well as two gems for my cuff links, paying $1,000 for the lot, about a quarter of what they were worth in the states.

When I was going through customs in Vietnam, I was told I had to leave the country. It was too dangerous. They shipped me right out of the airport, which was packed with people, planes, tanks, and warfare equipment. It reminded me of my time in the army as a sergeant, and I wanted to stay. I know it would have been interesting, but also unsafe so I left and went on to Hong Kong, where I joined Audrey at the exquisite Peninsula Hotel. Audrey wasn't allowed into Vietnam, so we met in Hong Kong. She remembers when I took her to meet my buddies, who were sitting with women.

"This is my wife," I said to them.

One replied, "Wife? Bringing your wife is like bringing a ham sandwich to a banquet!"

A Delightful French Invasion

I was getting ready to rehearse the orchestra in Hong Kong with our new addition to the show—the lovely French cabaret singer and movie star Denise Darcel. When I walked into the ballroom, I was shocked to hear the orchestra already playing. It seems that Denise had arrived before me and had handed the musicians the music she intended to use, along with instructions on how to play it.

I didn't hesitate, but walked to the front, immediately stopped the rehearsal cold, and made it clear to Denise that this orchestra already had a conductor, and it wasn't Denise Darcel. I then asked her to tell me how she wanted her music played.

She sulked for a while, until it was her turn to sing. After that, our roles were clear. She was so pleased with the rehearsal that she suggested we go to the roof garden and celebrate with champagne. Denise's husband, Bob Atkinson, was too tired to join us, and I was ready for bed myself, but she had a way of insisting. *"Poopy!"* That's what she called me. *"Let's go have some champagne!"* We had a great time, finishing two bottles. I never drink that much of anything, so it was a night to remember for me. By the time we headed back to our rooms you couldn't tell that Denise had anything to drink.

The next day Denise said she wanted to buy jewelry, and invited me along. I had gotten such a bargain the last time I went on a jewelry-hunting expedition that I agreed to go along. We went to a fabulous jewelry store, and she picked out a ring for herself while I chose one for Audrey. I made a deal with the jeweler to hold the ring as a surprise. It was quite a large round jade set in gold, with diamonds on the side. Later I brought Audrey to the jewelry store. The owner showed her many rings, but not the one I had picked out for her, until the end. When she saw that one, she was overwhelmed. We had been married a long time by then, and I wanted to give her something special.

To this day, my children call that ring our "eyeball." It's always part of the conversation when we talk about our trip to the Far East.

One of the things Audrey and I loved about Hong Kong were the balconies with tailors, who made your clothes on the spot. They measured you; the next day you went for a fitting; and on the third day your suits were ready, handmade, and first class. We both took advantage of this Hong Kong phenomenon.

Playing for the Armed Services Once More

The Hotel Manila in the Philippines was magnificent, overlooking the ocean and offering top-notch service. I played there, and one time the audience consisted of an Air Force Squadron, 150 men who had just completed a bombing raid in Vietnam. It was Easter time, and they came because they heard I was an American. At the end, they gave me all sorts of medals. They all wore a lot of them. Audrey and I wanted to go to Subic Bay, and one way of getting there was via pedicab. What an adventure. We saw a man on a donkey crossing the road carrying a gigantic wooden cross on a pilgrimage, an unforgettable scene.

We flew back to Tokyo and visited Russ Gary, who had married a Japanese girl. While we were sitting on the floor for a meal, in the customary way, there was an earthquake strong enough to rattle the dishes and us too.

The Japanese thought nothing of it. Russ's wife said, "It's just a slight tremor."

From Tokyo we went on to Hollywood, so I could visit the William Morris office that had booked me on this Far East tour. I spoke to the agency president, who told me to relax for a few days and then he would send me to Vegas.

When I told Audrey about his idea, she wasn't too happy. Neither was I. We missed our family and wanted to go home. I thanked the William Morris staff and we headed happily to the East Coast.

Chapter Twelve
Audrey's Road Trip Ends in Shangri La, Connecticut

WE WERE HAPPY TO BE HOME, but I was once again without a job. I had been away so long that it seemed everybody had forgotten the piano player. A friend, Selma Brody, with whom I had written some children's songs, recommended me for a job with a recording company, Ambassador Records, as A&R (Artists and Repertoire) man. Many A&R executives are musicians because they are responsible for discovering new recording artists and are expected to understand current market tastes and to find artists, often through word of mouth "on the street."

I produced my own piano album in a studio in Boston for Ambassador during this time. I had also done a few albums for Columbia and for Jubilee while I was on the Godfrey show, including some with a rhythm section.

It came time for that great voice, Vaughn Monroe, to cut an album for Ambassador, and after he came to the studio to record, I brought him to the house for a photo shoot. It was a terrific day.

I was trying to get Frank Sinatra Jr. to record with me at Ambassador, but we couldn't agree on the songs he'd sing. He wanted to sing the songs that belonged to his father, but my feeling was that those songs had been sung, and he should sing the songs of today for the young audience. I told him as much. But Frank Jr. was as stubborn as his father, whom I had known very well. I knew we'd never get to any accommodation. And, I was right.

After we arrived back home, Audrey received a call from her good friend Claire Bannister, who had just returned from London where she met with Gordon Fraser, a producer of distinguished greeting cards through a company he founded in 1938. Claire received permission to represent the Gordon Fraser line of cards in the United States but she couldn't do it alone, so she enlisted Audrey. Soon Audrey was spending a good deal of time on the road, covering a wide-ranging territory as an American representative for the Gordon Fraser Gallery.

Fraser, a prominent military man, was a fascinating character, a former bookseller and print dealer. Audrey tells a story about having dinner with him and a group, for which he insisted on choosing the wine. He chose one bottle for the group and another for himself alone! Naturally, Fraser chose all his greeting card designs and was the first to reproduce the old masters and original artwork in making his cards, a practice now widely imitated. There are not too many card companies whose archives are in the Victoria and Albert Museum, as Gordon Fraser's are. The company was taken over by Hallmark after Fraser died in an auto accident.

As fate would have it, Audrey's sales territory included Connecticut. One day her travels took her to Kent, a small country town with a few businesses along its Main Street. Searching for a place to have lunch, she found a small eating place of no consequence. Visions danced in her head, as she began to wonder if this picturesque little town, with its abandoned railroad station right in the middle, might just be the place to open a nice restaurant, perhaps including an upscale bar. She wondered where the people of Kent and surrounding areas could go when they wanted to dine out, or perhaps even socialize a bit with their neighbors?

When Audrey returned home, she told me where she had been and what she had envisioned. My reaction was, "Are you crazy? I lost $30,000 in the Caro's deal and am not about to risk another. The place may sound good, but forget it."

She predicted that I would feel that way, but wouldn't I just look at Kent and then decide?

I wasn't at all happy about it, but finally I said I would look, just to be fair, though I wouldn't promise anything. The following Sunday was a nice day, the weather was great, so we took a ride to Kent.

Audrey was right. Kent was a small town and very charming but, having been burned once by an investment, I was reluctant to try again. I argued that I was a professional pianist, not a waiter or manager. We talked some more, and finally Audrey reminded me that, as it stood then, I was on the road all the time and my kids hardly saw me.

"That's how I make my living," was my answer. Then I started to think, and decided she was right. I was a married man, a family man. What's the good of having a family if I can't enjoy it? Kids do many things as they are growing up, things that in your later years become sweet memories.

With that thought in mind, and maybe a little more of Audrey's persuasion, I finally agreed to go for it.

Kent Welcomes Us, Sort Of

It was 1972. The first thing we had to do was buy the ramshackle building across from the railroad station and renovate it, then we needed to hire an architect who could design a beautiful but practical building. Next, we had to come up with the funds. The local banks in Kent wouldn't consider talking to me. I was an outsider, an Italian, and a New Yorker. They didn't accept anyone but a local farmer with a hay field. I finally decided I could borrow money on my residence and on my insurance policy, perhaps empty our bank account, sell our stocks, and borrow some money from my family members. It was quite an accomplishment, but we were successful.

We finally had the money to open the restaurant.

I hired a local contractor named Bo White and his partner, Roger

Peet, and the architect, a young woman named Betty Bennett, who had lots of imagination. She really did a great job. We were all so pleased with her work.

It would take us a whole year to construct the restaurant and a small apartment above it. The apartment was necessary, because it would be impossible for me to commute from my home in Locust Valley to Kent each day to play in the restaurant. I asked some of the women from the real estate firm that sold me the property to finish off the curtains for the restaurant. They were generous with their help and excited about being involved in creating the first new establishment to come to town in a long time.

Beside farmers with cows and hay, Kent had only two small banks, a hardware store, a grocery store, a coffee shop that was run down, a library, a barbershop, a funeral home in an old house, and a lumber yard. This was the town of Kent, pop: 2,000 people.

With the restaurant finally completed, we moved to Kent and became residents without much fanfare but it took time before we were accepted and no longer regarded as "those New Yorkers."

Expert Pianist, Amateur Restaurateur

Locust Valley, where we lived before Kent, was the home of many CEOs of large corporations, and I received helpful advice from many of them. One executive, Ed Gallagher, had chaired the board at AT&T. Another, Ed Birkins, my next-door neighbor, was an officer at Lehman Brothers. I couldn't ask for more expert advice.

During the restaurant's construction, I received a phone call from an old friend, Al Flon, who had managed some of the largest restaurants in New York and Las Vegas. "You can't build and run a restaurant without me," he said. "You'll lose your shirt and go bankrupt. I'm coming up there to help you."

When I told him I couldn't afford him, he insisted that he was coming anyway. He did, and it's a good thing, because with what I knew about running a restaurant I would have gone broke in a short time.

I soon found out just how much has to be purchased before you set up a restaurant from scratch, things I knew nothing about, such as furniture, dinnerware, glassware, silverware, stoves, pots and pans, and a host of other things. The list seemed endless. If it weren't for Al to guide me in what was needed, who to see, and where to get supplies, it would have been impossible for us open.

Al's goal was to see me open as easily as possible. The day finally arrived when we had to order our food. That's when Al was particularly valuable. He knew where to get fresh fish, meat, vegetables, coffee, bread, and all the other essentials. He also had the linens, tables, tablecloths, and napkins delivered. I was so grateful that Al had volunteered himself; he was invaluable.

Chapter Thirteen
How the Fife 'n Drum Got Its Name

WE FINALLY SET A DATE to open our restaurant, and that meant everybody making a huge push to meet that date.

One night Audrey and I were at a cocktail party in New Fairfield, a neighboring town, with a bunch of friends, including Wally Griffin, He was a popular singer and humorist, who appeared frequently at Ruby Foo's as well as on Carol Channing's cast albums and *The Ed Sullivan Show,* where he often joined a lineup of the very best names in the business.

Naturally, our friends at the party were asking the name of our restaurant. We had to admit we didn't yet have one. Fortunately, we were with a group of creative people who wouldn't allow our new restaurant to stay nameless for long.

They started to think aloud. The name had to be musical, said Wally, and the location is New England, so it's got to sound New English, they agreed. The site of the restaurant is a pre-Revolutionary village. With a few more drinks all around, the collective effort quickly paid off.

Music + American Revolution + New England = The Fife 'n Drum!

A Great Start on an Overflowing Opening Night

Opening night at the Fife 'n Drum, January 20, 1973, was a great success. People came from all over. The place was packed; there wasn't a seat to be had. I had purchased a Steinway piano from an old friend, Halcyon Hirschthal, and placed it in the center of the restaurant. I played my tail off that evening.

I had designed a ledge around the piano, with the help of Hunt's furniture over in nearby Dutchess County, New York. I showed them what I needed and they did exactly as I sketched on a pad. To this day, it serves the same purpose as it did that opening night.

Lots of good friends sat around the piano that first night, including Bill Tobin, the Sunoco station owner; Gordon Casey, from the real estate agency; Gene Bull, the postmaster; Leo Rosati, the construction contractor; Bob Smith and his wife Pattie; Ron Klein and his wife, who published a magazine in Danbury; and Johnny Gawel, whose automobile dealership was across the street from the restaurant.

They drank and sang until I stopped playing at 1 a.m.

The apartment I built above the restaurant proved to be a godsend, since I could stay there during the week. Audrey came up on weekends from our home in Locust Valley and hosted in the restaurant.

Creating a Homestead Next Door

The elderly woman who owned the property next door to the restaurant regularly visited us at the Fife. In 1974 she took ill and was being cared for by her niece. Some weeks later, she passed away. At the funeral I asked her niece what would become of the property. She told me it had been willed by her father to a church in Brooklyn and was scheduled to revert to the church. If I were interested in the property, she suggested I contact the church pastor.

I called the pastor and asked if the church would be interested in selling. He said he'd think about it. About a week later, he called and said yes, they would sell it. He gave me what seemed like a fair price. I accepted his offer and we closed the deal. The property consisted of an old Victorian house and about three acres of land on Route 7.

We sold the house on Piping Rock Road in Locust Valley, New York and moved into the house next door to the restaurant.

We love the place.

Eric Sloane Feels Right at Home

Eric Sloane, one of the most important landscape artists from the Hudson River School of painting, spent quite a bit of time at the Fife 'n Drum. Born in New York City, he lived nearby in the Merryall area of New Milford, CT, though I had known him earlier in Locust Valley.

What a fascinating history he had! Eric Sloane wasn't his name at all. It was Everard Jean Hinrichs until some of his early painting teachers advised him that experienced painters changed their names so they wouldn't have to take the blame for their youthful, inferior works. He had traveled across the nation when he was twenty, making his living as a sign painter. He loved our nation's landscape so much, he lifted the E-R-I-C from the middle of "America" and took it for a first name. "Sloane" is the name of his mentor, with an "e" added.

He developed an impressive collection of historic tools that became the basis of the historic collection in Kent's Sloane-Stanley Museum. As the author of several distinguished books on the subject, Eric had a deep interest in New England culture, especially Colonial daily life, so he was a natural fan of the Fife 'n Drum, where he is honored.

When you arrive at the Fife, the Eric Sloane Room is just to the right where the walls are decorated with Artist Proofs signed by Eric. The beamed, low-ceiling dining room is typical of the early 1900s, a perfect choice for Eric's room. Eric came every night for dinner, and, in a sense, adopted me. He loved to hear me play the piano, often inviting his friends.

The Armstrong Genius Graces Our Walls

A few years after we opened, Eric Sloane teamed up with brilliant landscape painter David Armstrong, his friend and protégé, to create a three-story panoramic mural for the National Air and Space Museum. David, also a neighbor, was another treasured friend who loved the Fife, and whose works grace the walls in yet another room. It was rare for David to come for dinner without saying, "Here's a present for you."

Each gift would be another of his outstanding paintings. He eventually gifted us enough to fill the walls of the Fife's front room, making it the David Armstrong room.

These marvelous prints are a tribute to Kent. Several are renderings of David's favorite local spots in and around town, such as "Numeral Rock" and "Preservation," while the portraits are of people the artist grew up with. "The Old Man" is his father, Bill Armstrong, legendary master at Kent School. Then there's "Eric Sloane" and "Bart Segar," a portrait of the heir to the 200-acre dairy on Kent's Segar Mountain Road.

America's Tough Guy in a Tender Mood

James Cagney, a friend of Eric's, lived in nearby New York State where a major road is named for him. Whenever Jimmy came in, I played songs from some of his movies and Broadway shows. When these songs ended, I would find Jimmy with tears in his eyes.

One night, an elderly woman asked if that was Jimmy Cagney at the table over there. When I replied that it was, she asked if she could meet him. When I mentioned it to Jimmy, he followed me over to her table. After exchanging a few pleasantries with her, he said, "Madame, may I have this dance?"

And, with that, he took her hand and escorted her to the dance floor. I'll bet that woman never stopped talking about that night.

Jimmy once invited me to his house for dinner. He had also invited a few of the stars he knew and had worked with, like Pat O'Brien, and thought I would enjoy meeting them.

Jimmy Cagney and I became good friends. I cried when he passed away.

The Wild Bunch Gathers at the Fife

Sometimes when Eric Sloane came in at night he would ask if Paul Newman had been there. When I would say "no," Eric would say, again, that he'd bring Paul one night for dinner. Finally he did. Not only did Paul Newman come in but also he brought his entire crew from Lime Rock Racetrack with him. Sometimes Paul came in with his racing partner, Bob Sharp.

Paul Newman was a skilled race driver. The Racing Association wanted him to quit at age seventy-five but he refused and continued racing until he was almost eighty. Paul had a great track record, literally. When he died, he left the profits from his food company to charity. He was a special kind of person. There are few of his type around and those who knew Paul miss him very much.

Robert Redford was unassuming, at least when he came to the Fife. He was so laid back that he once stayed in his car to read a script for a new movie while his family ate dinner.

Richard Widmark visited us with friends from his home in Roxbury. Richard had a hearing problem. Whenever he came in, I would discreetly stop playing for a while, so he could converse with his friends as they dined.

Gregory Peck was also unassuming and I liked him. Arthur Miller, married at that time to Marilyn Monroe, came in with theater friends. They might have been famous, but I don't remember that they impressed me very much.

A Familiar Deep Voice in My Living Room

Henry Kissinger was doing a lot of early morning television interviews during the seventies. At one point, his house was being renovated and the TV station asked for permission to use our living room as the temporary TV studio. They thought our house had the perfect appeal for such a broadcast. The crew arrived early in the morning and set up in the living room, just as they would have done in a TV studio. Preparing and broadcasting the shows generally took all morning, so I would talk to Dr. Kissinger while I was having breakfast. We all know him as having a basso, gravelly voice, but many would be surprised at how down-to-earth he is.

I once asked if he thought the crisis in the Middle East would be settled. He didn't think so. Thirty years have passed without peace, so I guess Dr. Kissinger knew what he was talking about.

James Taylor used to come in with his wife, Carly Simon. Turns out that his manager at the time, Shelly Schultz, a well-known booking agent, had also been my agent when I signed with William Morris. They owned a gorgeous piece of property on the edge of town, overlooking the mountains.

Eric Sloane would bring in Dustin Hoffman, who talked about his movies at great length, telling fascinating stories about his early days as an actor in Hollywood, and the tough time he had getting started. He was particularly proud of *Tootsie*. I met Dustin while he was walking in Hyannis with his children. I asked him what he was doing up there, and he said nothing in particular; he just wanted his children to see what the Cape looked like. He is a good father.

Ed and Pegeen Spread the Word

I was on KMOX, a local radio station during much of this time. Peter Drake was my announcer, teamed up with the talented engineer and sound effects man, Ham O'Hara. We did a half-hour show and invited celebrities who were performing in the area. I played several solos during the show and accompanied the guest entertainers.

Two of the New York area's most beloved radio personalities for many decades, both in the city and here in Kent, were Ed and Pegeen Fitzgerald, whose daily broadcast on radio station WOR was a radio institution for forty-two years, with two million listeners. The tagline of their popular show, *The Fitzgeralds,* was "Book Talk, Back Talk, and Small Talk." Like Arthur Godfrey, Ed and Pegeen read their own commercials in a casual way, so their show always sounded like a friendly, fascinating conversation going on between the two of them, one liberal and one conservative.

The Fife 'n Drum restaurant had now become home to many celebrities, and Ed would call me each morning to ask who had come into the Fife the previous night. I would give him names of artists, actors, musicians and celebrities whom I'd played for the night before, and he'd mention them on the air. It was great publicity for us, and fun for Ed. He died in 1982 and Pegeen died in 1989. They were also famous for their love for cats; she started The Last Post, a highly regarded no-kill shelter still operating in Sharon, Connecticut.

Everything but the Bleachers

When Billy Martin, the baseball player, came for dinner, our restaurant was mobbed with his fans. You would think you were at Yankee Stadium, from the size of the crowd that came to see Billy.

Lynn Redgrave, a great lady from one of England's leading theater families, visited us. Lynne came to Kent to live but also chose our town as her home during her last days; Kent loved and protected her through her last illness. She was so generous in sharing her talent, performing locally as powerfully as if she were on Broadway.

Mia Farrow, who had been married to Frank Sinatra for a couple of years in the late sixties, lived nearby. She came into the Fife while on theater tour with her mother, the actress, Maureen O'Sullivan, and

Lucille Ball, who needs no introduction.

I ran into Mia again after Eric Sloane asked me to go with him to New York City for an award ceremony. He said, "I don't want to sit on that dais alone with a bunch of strangers." I went with him, and one of the people on the dais was Mia Farrow, who said I looked familiar. Many years before, she had come to the Fife with her mother and Lucille Ball, so I reminded her.

We often see our neighbor Bob Avian for dinner, sometimes with Patti LuPone, bringing Broadway to Kent. We are so proud of Bob around here, and we love the show business stories he tells so well. An amazing choreographer, he collaborated with Michael Bennett on history-making shows, including *Company, Follies, Ballroom, Dreamgirls,* and *A Chorus Line,* which was revived in 2006, with Bob directing.

Meryl Streep had just finished making the movie *Julia,* about Julia Child, when she came in one evening. It turns out that Chef Yves Labe, Julia Child's assistant on her cooking show, was the same chef I'd brought to the U.S. from Paris for the Fife 'n Drum. Unfortunately, I wasn't able to keep Yves. He went to work at a fine—ultimately Five Star—French restaurant in Boca Raton. While he was with me, though, the French chefs in the area would come to have dinner with him and discuss our menu. That was always an impressive gathering.

After Yves left, we began a search for a new chef. We interviewed many, but couldn't come up with what we were seeking until my maitre d' brought in a friend he'd worked with in New York City. The chef was Lubomir Pecorina. I hired him and he stayed with me for thirty-five years until I convinced him it was time for both of us to retire.

It was a great joy to meet another neighbor, one of the leading violinists of the world, Isaac Stern, when he came to the Fife for lunch or dinner, which he did frequently. He loved to listen to me play while he ate, sometimes glancing through a newspaper during his meal, but clearly listening at the same time.

I felt truly honored.

The life-changing connection I had with Arturo Toscanini decades earlier was not to be the last contact I would have with that family.

Wanda Toscanini Horowitz was a force of nature. Daughter of Arturo Toscanini and wife of Vladimir Horowitz, she had studied piano and voice as a child but did not pursue a career in music, fearing she would never be able to live up to her father's famously exacting standards. She loved to visit the Fife 'n Drum from her nearby home.

When I told her I had attended Juilliard because her father had recommended me, she said, "Well, he must have been *very* impressed with your playing!"

Wanda Toscanini Horowitz was known as the only person who would stand up to her father. And not only to her father. As the story goes, she once spotted Virgil Thomson, the celebrated composer and critic, dozing during a Toscanini concert. Fully aware that Thomson frequently gave her father negative reviews, she went over to him and announced, "I am Wanda Toscanini Horowitz, and I saw you sleep from the first note to the last. I hope you enjoyed the performance."

A famously tough critic herself, she showed her approval of my performances at the Fife by offering me the ultimate compliment. Referring to her husband by the name that close friends and family called him, she said, "When Volodya hears you play, he's going to love you."

Fully aware that she was talking about a musical legend, perhaps the greatest living pianist, I could be forgiven for not entirely sharing her confidence.

But Mrs. Horowitz was right. Several nights later, she came in with the great man himself. I played, as usual, though that night I was nervous, which is understandable. But I needn't have been—he loved my playing so much that he asked me to sit with him while he ate, asking me about my piano studies and my teachers at Juilliard. He knew them all! He also gave me great comfort by telling me that all pianists get nervous performing before others.

We talked quite a bit, and became friends. It was a tremendous feeling to have gained the approval of the very best of the best.

My favorite moments were when I would be playing the piano, while noticing in my peripheral vision that Vladimir Horowitz was happily conducting my performance, right there at the table, between the soup and the entree.

My Last, Great, Dolph Traymon Trio

After a while we built up enough of a weekend audience of jazz fans at the Fife 'n Drum for me to form another trio. Nothing but the best would do for my own restaurant, so I reached out to two of the finest musicians I knew, and they said yes.

Our drummer, Buddy Christian, had played with the Harry James and Ina Ray Hutton bands. We were all playing well until one day he and my bass player had a disagreement; Buddy opted to quit the trio and go home to spend the rest of his time fishing from the boat he always carried on the roof of his car. I didn't want this to happen, obviously, and warned Buddy that if he didn't change his mind I'd report him to the musicians' union. He knew what that could mean, so he patched up his quarrel with our bassist, who was no ordinary bassist.

He was Leonard Gaskin, who had backed up Ella Fitzgerald for several years, and had taken Oscar Pettiford's spot in Dizzy Gillespie's band. He'd also played with Cootie Williams, Charlie Parker, Erroll Garner and other greats, including Eddie Condon, Stan Getz, Miles Davis, and Lady Day herself, Billie Holiday.

We had a good time working together.

The Dolph Traymon Trio at the Fife 'n Drum made our audiences very happy. Lenny died in 2009 and Buddy died shortly afterward. Rather than form a new group, I decided to perform solo and work fewer hours.

It's not the same. I sure miss those guys.

Chapter Fourteen

A Toast from Moët, and Dolph Traymon Day

WRITING THIS MEMOIR brings to mind so many happy events in my long life and one very sad time.

My mind goes back to the day before my sixty-second birthday, November 26, 1982, when I received a phone call from my brother, Joe, telling me that our mother was dying and that if I wanted to see her I must come quickly.

Audrey and I dressed rapidly and raced to the hospital, but Mother had passed away just a few minutes before we arrived. My mother had been my most ardent supporter, and always talked about her "famous son."

I wasn't famous, but she seemed to think so and was proud of me. She would tell people, "You have to hear my son play."

She may be gone, but I think of her often, and I still feel the loss after all these years. It's funny how, as you get older, you tend to draw closer to your family. My sister is gone now too; my brother Joe and I are the only ones left of our immediate family. I try to talk to him often.

As a tribute to my mother, I visited the home town she and my father shared, during our trip to Europe. The trip was launched by a tribute to the Fife 'n Drum from the French winery, Moët, an honor that would have made my mother proud.

First on My List: Great Wines for the Fife

From the day the Fife opened its doors, I was determined to become a wine connoisseur and to work hard to create a superb wine list. We succeeded. Our wine list was eventually considered one of the best in the state of Connecticut, and in 1990, Moët and Chandon acknowledged that. They invited Audrey and me to Paris for a special luncheon and wine tasting at Epernay, the home of their champagne winery.

We were among fourteen guests, among them the heads of French wineries and of Louis Vuitton, the fashion house. The luncheon, served by four waiters, was superb, of course, and the Moët and Chandon executives went out of their way to make us feel honored and important.

It was fascinating to be taken to the Moët winery to see how fine champagne is made from the first pressing of white grapes, aged in casks from five to seven years before bottling, while Dom Perignon is aged eight years.

We followed up that intriguing visit with a trip to the Louvre, and then to lunch—we thought—at the Eiffel Tower. Though I had phoned for a reservation from the US, it was not honored. It was my seventieth birthday, and I would like to have celebrated it there, but it was not to be. Disappointed, I told Audrey, "They can keep their erector set," which is what I thought of the Eiffel Tower at that moment.

Instead, we enjoyed a wonderful meal near our hotel, and the waiter informed us that what happened to our reservation was all too common. We managed to enjoy the beautiful, vibrant city of Paris that night.

A More Important Reservation Honored

As long as we were in Europe, we wanted to see Rome, since some of my father's people called that city home, and I thought it would be nice to visit them. We took a taxi to the address I had been given, and an elderly lady named Romanina answered the door, saying that my cousin Gabriella would be home from her job at the airline, Al'Italia, soon. Gabriella took us to dinner and sent us on a picturesque bus tour.

I had contacted the Vatican, asking for an audience with Pope John XXIII, and so we took a taxi to the Vatican. There I told the priest in charge that I had sent a request by telegram, but had received no response. He rummaged through papers on a desk and came back with my request, telling us we were in the group scheduled for the next day, and suggesting what we should wear: a suit and tie for me and a long-sleeved dress, gloves, and a hat for Audrey.

Several hundred people were in the audience the next day. An elderly Polish woman next to me got a kiss on the forehead from the Holy Father.

It was an emotional experience for all of us.

St. Peter's Cathedral and the Sistine Chapel were both inspiring— so much more powerful than their photographs can capture. We saw the Catacombs and the Vatican Museum, with its early Roman ruins, and Roman baths, as well as the Villa d'Este where we were caught in a downpour, complete with hailstones.

That afternoon I paid tribute to my art with a visit to the house where Franz Liszt wrote one of his concertos.

Sentimental Journey to Mother's Hometown

My mother's family came from the same little town in the province of Calabria where my father was raised. As I mentioned earlier, Scilla is a small seacoast village on the Adriatic Sea. Eager to see the town that means so much to my family, Audrey and I traveled there by train, stopping at Reggio, the nearest station. Upon our arrival, we followed a sign that read *albergo*, which means hotel in Italian. That led us to a small rustic hotel. After checking in and freshening up, we asked the owner how to get to Scilla. Pointing to the road in front of the station, he said, "Follow that road up to the top of the hill. That is Scilla."

On a pleasant day in early afternoon, we walked up the hill, which ended in a piazza (plaza). Off to one side was a stone wall, three feet high, overlooking a beach and facing the Strait of Messina.

Opposite the wall was a café with a group of tables set outside. We ordered a gelato and an espresso, and the waiter, surmising we were American, asked us what we were doing there. When I told him my mother was born there and we had relatives there, and that one of them was Dr. Panucchio, he disappeared into the restaurant. In short order, one of my cousins, a brother of Dr. Panucchio, appeared.

He insisted that we visit his mother, my mother's Aunt Elena, that night. Dr. Panucchio was there and we had dinner with him. He was head doctor at the hospital we visited the next day. He told us it had been built and equipped with money from friends and relatives in the US.

A Royal Welcome Home

After topping off our trip by visiting the wonderful cities of Milan and Bologna, we returned home to be treated like royalty, with our children and several friends greeting us like long-lost world travelers.

To my surprise, then-Governor Lowell Weicker called and said he was coming to the restaurant for dinner. I was glad to see him. When we lived in Locust Valley, and I was seeking work for my band by contacting various charities that regularly planned functions, Governor Weicker's sister-in-law, then his secretary, was instrumental in giving me recommendations. We did very well, with her help.

One afternoon, at the age of eighty-two, I was approached by the president of the Kent Lions Club. He asked if I would play a concert to benefit the Club. I thought seriously about it since I had started the club and was its first charter president.

We performed the concert on September 29, 2002, and raised about $3,500. My family, some of my close friends, and many admirers came from all over. It was an undeniable success. Many guests, who had been to the concert, came to dinner with us at the Fife that night to express their pleasure once again.

I had recorded a special CD for that concert to benefit the school fund. We sold several hundred CDs that night. I felt I had accomplished something worthwhile for the school as well as for the town. Marvelwood had been like a stepchild in comparison to the Kent School, which had received vastly more publicity over the years. But Marvelwood has since grown, and is now recognized on its own merits, including the addition of a fantastic new gymnasium.

In 2004 I was asked by Thomas Sebring, a friend who is on the school board, to do another concert at Marvelwood School, to benefit students who wanted to study but lacked the funds. I did so, and once again, we had a fine turnout. Many months after the concert, I received a letter from a family in the Midwest, thanking me for the music lessons their son received from the school as a result of my concert. I sat down and cried when I received the letter, thrilled that this child received such a benefit from my concert.

Dolph Traymon Day in Connecticut

I never considered myself to be a concert pianist although my fans seem to have other ideas. Though I was almost ninety years old, the Lions Club asked me to do yet another benefit concert, this one at the Kent School on February 8, 2009. It was planned for mid-afternoon on a Sunday in order to get the best possible attendance. About 400 people attended.

At the end of my concert, State Senator Andrew Roraback presented me with a plaque, signed by Governor Jodie Rell proclaiming February 8, 2009 as DOLPH TRAYMON DAY.

What a high honor this was for me and my family. I never dreamed anything like a Dolph Traymon Day could happen and I appreciated it no end. It was a great payoff for all my years of practicing and sacrificing.

The piano has certainly given me a great life!

Photos this page by Karen Chase

Acknowledgements

IN RETROSPECT, I have had a very good life indeed. As my wife, Audrey, puts it, "We'll never die wondering." I have also been blessed with a wonderful, caring family—both the one I was born into and the one Audrey and I raised.

Our eldest daughter, Elissa, has been managing the restaurant for quite a few years, and is known throughout Kent, not only for her efficiency but for her grace. Our customers tell us they deeply appreciate the charming way she greets each of them, welcoming both new and old with equal warmth. Elissa is directly responsible for the Fife 'n Drum still being very much alive and well after all these years.

Elissa and her husband, George Potts, who is like a son to us, raised two lovely daughters. Kate, the eldest, has blessed us with three delightful great grandchildren, Charlotte, Wyatt, and Will. Sarah, their younger daughter, is a remarkable young woman who has traveled all over Europe, Africa, and parts of Asia. Sarah will soon marry Mike Ashton, a rising young Hollywood filmmaker.

Our younger daughter, Tracey, is a vice-president in the Trust Division of the global Deutsche Bank. Her husband, Cliff Whitehead, is also like a son to us. As busy as Tracey is, she's always had time to come to the Fife's rescue on many occasions. She's even been known to take over in the kitchen when we were between chefs. You can often find Tracey and her wonderful daughter, Morgan, a student at Springfield College, helping Elissa with private parties as well as at the restaurant, from time to time.

Audrey and I agree, *this* is the real proof of our success, our loving, devoted—and growing—family.

Our extraordinary Fife 'n Drum staff is much appreciated by our family and our customers. They work unfailingly, always with style and good humor. Our customers truly love them, and we are fortunate to have them.

We're grateful to St. Andrew's Episcopal Church, our spiritual community in Kent, and our inspiring Rector, Rev. Roger B. White, for his kindness and his guidance.

From the Top: The Dolph Traymon Story would not have been possible without the existence of the earlier edition of this book, transcribed by my brother, Joseph Tramontana, with the assistance of Louise Santos. Thank you!

My sister Adele's extensively researched family chronicle, written in 1989, has been absolutely invaluable.

Last, but not least, thanks to Patricia Horan of Kent's Round House Press for putting it all together and making my life an enjoyable read.